CLOUD COMPUTING FUNDAMENTALS

INTRODUCTION TO MICROSOFT AZURE AZ-900 EXAM

RICHIE MILLER

Disclaimer

Every effort was made to produce this book as truthful as possible, but no warranty is implied. The author shall have neither liability nor responsibility to any person or entity concerning any loss or damages ascending from the information contained in this book. The information in the following pages are broadly considered to be truthful and accurate of facts, and such any negligence, use or misuse of the information in question by the reader will render any resulting actions solely under their purview.

Table of Contents

Introduction

In the following chapters, we're going to talk about the AZ-900 exam and how to prepare for it. We will first cover the benefits of getting Azure certified and why you should consider getting the AZ-900 certification. We will then do an overview of the AZ-900 certification exam, what you will be evaluated on, as well as learn about the skills measured document. Finally, we will do an overview of our learning materials for this exam. By the end of this book, you will know what's needed to start studying for the AZ-900 Microsoft Certification exam. Let's start by learning what are the benefits of getting Azure certified and, more particular, why the AZ-900 exam. Let's start by asking, why do we even want to get a Microsoft certification? First of all, Microsoft certifications can really help give you a professional advantage by providing globally recognized and industry-endorsed evidence of mastering skills in a digital and cloud business. If we look at the numbers, according to multiple studies, 91% of certified IT professionals say that certification gives them more professional credibility, 93% of decision makers agree that certified employees provide more added value, and 52% of certified IT professionals say that their expertise is more sought after within the organization after getting certified. Honestly, certifications can also help you in the financial aspect of your career. 35% of technical professionals say that getting certified led to salary or wage increases, while 26% of technical professionals reported job promotions after getting certified. Now let's get a bit more Azure-specific and talk why we want to get Azure certified. Microsoft Azure is one of the top cloud providers in the world for Infrastructure and Platform as Service workloads. 63% of enterprises in the world are currently running apps on Microsoft Azure, second only to AWS. However, 19% of enterprises expect to invest significantly more on Azure in 2022, and this is leading all of the other cloud vendors this year, so Azure is still growing at an astonishing rate. Finally, 44.5% of enterprises say that Microsoft Azure is their preferred provider for cloud business intelligence. If we get more specific into our Azure certification, the Azure certification portfolio is actually the biggest certification portfolio at Microsoft, and it includes 3 fundamental-level certifications, 10 associate-level certifications, 2 expert-level certifications, and 3 specialty-level certifications. But what makes the AZ-900 unique? The AZ-900 Azure Fundamental Certification is an optional, but very highly recommended prerequisite for all of the other Azure certifications. It's the place you should start whether you have done a Microsoft certification before and now you want to specialize in Azure, or if this is your first ever Microsoft certification, the AZ-900 is where you should begin your Azure certification journey.

Chapter 1 AZ-900 Exam Summary

Now that we know why the AZ-900 is a very important and valuable exam, let's do an overview of the exam. The Azure Fundamental Certification is an opportunity to prove knowledge of cloud concepts, Azure services, Azure workloads, security and privacy in Azure, as well as Azure pricing and support. From an audience point of view, the AZ-900 is intended for candidates who are just beginning to work with cloud-based solutions and services or are new to Azure. Also, as this is a fundamentals exam, before starting to study, candidates should be familiar with general technology concepts, but really no other requirements as you will learn the fundamentals in the study material for this exam. If we take a look at the basics, the AZ-900 exam costs 99 USD; however, the price might vary depending on your region. Furthermore, I highly encourage you to check with your manager or HR person as organizations will often reimburse the cost for learning and certifications. The worst that they can say is no, so it's always worth to ask. Also, something that is really nice is that fundamental certifications do not expire. For example, associate and expert-level Microsoft certifications expire after one year, but because this is a fundamentals-level exam, it doesn't expire, so that is nice. Lastly, if you're a student, you can actually get college credit for passing Microsoft exams and earning Microsoft certifications. This works mostly in the United States, not internationally. If we take a look at the skills measured, it's split up into six categories, the first one being describe cloud concepts, which is 20 to 25% of the exam. We then have describe core Azure services, which is 15 to 20% of the exam. Third, we have to describe core solutions and management tools on Azure, which is 10 to

15% of the exam. Fourth, we have to describe general security and network security features, which is between 10 and 15% of the exam. Our fifth category is describing identity, governance, privacy, and compliance features, which is 20 to 25% of the exam. Finally, describe Azure cost management and service-level agreements, which is between 10 to 15% of the exam. There is one keyword that is repeated throughout each objective, and that is the verb describe. Verbs are very important in Microsoft certifications. So, what does the word describe mean? As we're talking about the fundamentals-level exam, the verb describe tells us that you do not need to know how to configure, manage or implement features. What you really need to know is what features are available and what business problems they solve. The goal of this exam is for you to be able to know what cloud computing challenges can be solved by what Azure solution. If you talk with someone and they say we have this business need for a workload, you need to be able to know, this Azure solution can help you with that. This is why the AZ-900 is an amazing exam for anyone working in the Microsoft ecosystem. Whether you're an IT pro, dev, project manager or business stakeholder, knowing what solutions Microsoft offers can really allow you to better understand the projects you're working on and to propose the right solution at the right time. Now that we have talked about the high-level objectives, Microsoft also provides a document called the skills outline, or the skills measured document, and it's important to review it before and after studying for this exam. The skills outlined are the full detailed list of everything that you need to know for the exam. We will review it later, but really this should be our checklist of things to study for the AZ-900 exams.

Chapter 2 Skills Measured Document

If you open up your browser and type AZ-900, this page will be one of the first choices.

This is the Microsoft Learning page for the AZ-900 Microsoft Azure Fundamentals exam. On the exam page at the top, you will see the description and audience for the exam, you will be able to schedule it, but what we want to talk about is the skills measured.

Skills measured

- The content of this exam was updated on November 9, 2020. Please download the exam skills outline below to see what changed.
- Describe cloud concepts (20-25%)
- Describe core Azure services (15-20%)
- Describe core solutions and management tools on Azure (10-15%)
- Describe general security and network security features (10-15%)
- Describe identity, governance, privacy, and compliance features (20-25%)
- Describe Azure cost management and Service Level Agreements (10-15%)

↓ Download exam skills outline

You will see on the exam page, you only have the high-level skills; however, it's important that you click this link, Download exam skills outline. If you click on it, it will open up a PDF, either it will download it or open up directly in the browser depending on your settings.

Exam AZ-900: Microsoft Azure Fundamentals – Skills Measured

This exam was updated on November 9, 2020. Following the current exam guide, we have included a version of the exam guide with Track Changes set to "On," showing the changes that were made to the exam on that date.

Audience Profile

Candidates for this exam should have foundational knowledge of cloud services and how those services are provided with Microsoft Azure. The exam is intended for candidates who are just beginning to work with cloud-based solutions and services or are new to Azure.

Azure Fundamentals exam is an opportunity to prove knowledge of cloud concepts, Azure

Something that is really important, because as the cloud always changes, so do Microsoft certification exams, so you might see at the top a warning like this one. This exam was updated on November 9, 2020, and if you go to the bottom, at the bottom you will have kind of a document with tracked changes on, so you can see what were the changes that were done on the date that it was changed.

NOTE: Most questions cover features that are General Availability (GA). The exam may contain questions on Preview features if those features are commonly used.

Describe Cloud Concepts (~~15~~ 2020 25%)

~~Identify~~ Describe the benefits and considerations of using cloud services

- identify the benefits of cloud computing, ~~Describe terms~~ such as High Availability, Scalability, Elasticity, Agility, ~~Fault Tolerance,~~ and Disaster Recovery
- ~~describe the principles of economies of scale~~
- ~~describe~~ Identify the differences between Capital Expenditure (CapEx) and Operational Expenditure (OpEx)
- describe the consumption-based model

Describe the differences between categories of cloud services~~Infrastructure-as-a-Service (IaaS), Platform-as-a-Service (PaaS) and Software-as-a-Service (SaaS)~~

- describe the shared responsibility model
- describe Infrastructure-as-a-Service (IaaS),

And Microsoft generally also announces at least one or two months in advance if a change will happen, and it will be shown the exact same way, simply the date will be on the future so you can see if Microsoft will change the objectives. If you go to the top, you have the Audience Profile again, same thing, but what gets interesting is that for each exam objective, so let's say Describe Cloud Concepts, it's broken down into sub-objectives and details. Under Describe Cloud Concepts, we have Identify the benefits and considerations of using cloud services, identify the benefits of cloud computing such as high availability, scalability, elasticity, agility, and disaster recovery.

Describe Cloud Concepts (20-25%)

Identify the benefits and considerations of using cloud services

- identify the benefits of cloud computing, such as High Availability, Scalability, Elasticity, Agility, and Disaster Recovery
- identify the differences between Capital Expenditure (CapEx) and Operational Expenditure (OpEx)
- describe the consumption-based model

Describe the differences between categories of cloud services

- describe the shared responsibility model
- describe Infrastructure-as-a-Service (IaaS),
- describe Platform-as-a-Service (PaaS)

Then we have to describe the differences between the categories of cloud services.

Describe the differences between categories of cloud services

- describe the shared responsibility model
- describe Infrastructure-as-a-Service (IaaS),
- describe Platform-as-a-Service (PaaS)

- describe serverless computing
- describe Software-as-a-Service (SaaS)
- identify a service type based on a use case

Describe the differences between types of cloud computing

So you need to know what's the difference between Infrastructure as a Service and Platform as a Service and Software as a Service and then identify a service type based on a use case, so, you need to be able to know what workloads should go where. Then for each objective really, you have all of the details on what services do you need to know, what are the different things you should be able to describe. You can either save it locally or you can even print it and then use a highlighter, once you feel confident you learned something, highlight it, and this should be the checklist for your exam. You need to be able to go in the details in the skills measured document and then be able to say that all of the different tools, services, and concepts in here, I'm able to describe. It's an important tool for your study to pass the AZ-900 exam.

Chapter 3 Why Use Microsoft Azure

We're going to look at a lot of individual services within Azure throughout the book, but in this chapter, I want to give you a broad overview of what Azure can do and how it's structured. I'm going to demystify Azure for you and give you the bigger picture of the environment that all the individual services operate in before we go into many of those services later on. But first, I want to talk about the Azure Fundamentals certification. If you're studying for the AZ-900 exam, this book will definitely help you do that, but this book doesn't encompass all of the exam objectives. If you're studying for the exam, I encourage you to read the most up-to-date study guide provided by Microsoft because it does change from time to time and then map those objectives to the topics covered in this book. That way, you'll be able to see what else you need to learn outside of this book in order to pass the exam. That said, this is a book for people new to Azure, so we're going to start from the ground up by talking about why you would want to use Azure in the first place. Azure is a cloud platform with more than 200 products and services that help you create applications and solutions. The cloud platform part just means that Microsoft abstracts away all the underlying hosting infrastructure so you can rent basic things like web hosting, computing power, databases, and storage, as well as some really full-featured solutions, like business analytics tools, artificial intelligence services, and portals for managing devices for the Internet of Things. You might never use some of those advanced tools, but they give you options you probably didn't have on-premises, at least not without installing a bunch of software and services on your own servers to do those things. But even if you just host websites and file shares, traditional things that every organization does, why would you want to use Azure? Well, there's a lot that goes into managing your own servers and datacenter. There's buying the physical hardware, storing those servers in a secure place where nobody can tamper with them, there's cooling needed because servers generate a lot of heat, and there's electricity and of course backup electricity unless you don't mind your applications being unavailable during a power outage, plus all the networking components and monitoring for health, as well as to make sure that no one hacks your network and computers. But there's also less obvious things, like you might have a need for a lot of computing power at certain times of the day, week or year, so you need the servers to be able to handle that load. Let's say you're hosting an ecommerce application to sell your company's products and there's way more traffic around Christmas than during the rest of the year. You need your servers to be able to handle the load, but they sit underutilized the rest of the year. That's a waste of money and hard drives can fail or you might need to keep increasing your storage because the business groups keep generating more files. They tend to do that. Then they're storing backups of files and databases. What about disaster recovery? If there's a major outage at your datacenter, are you okay with the apps not being available or do you want to maintain another datacenter in another location that can take over that traffic? There's also the ongoing maintenance of the operating systems on those servers. They need to be patched and monitored for threats. Then every five years or so, you need to replace all that hardware, not to mention the networking components like routers, switches, and firewalls. Microsoft, Azure and cloud computing in general was created to address many of these issues. For the rest of this book, we'll look at services in Azure for hosting applications and data and all the virtual infrastructure that allows you to do that. You'll see how easy it is to create and configure that infrastructure in Azure without having to manage any physical hardware like you do on-premises. We'll start with signing up for a subscription in Azure. That'll give you a way to follow along and create your own Azure services. Then you'll start to learn how Azure is implemented using regions, how those regions are connected, and all about Azure datacenters in the regions. You'll learn about resource groups, which are the containers for holding multiple resources that make up a logical grouping, like for an application. Then we'll explore the Azure portal, which is the main way you'll be interacting with Azure and managing instances of services that you create. We'll create some resources in the portal, and I'll show you Azure Active Directory, which is the identity service in Azure for managing user accounts, and it provides the foundation for access control for managing Azure, as well as access control for the people using the applications that you deploy to Azure. Finally, we'll tie a lot of the Azure concepts together by discussing how Azure Active Directory and subscriptions are related. So let's get started by signing up for an Azure subscription next.

Chapter 4 How to Create an Azure Subscription

Let's create an Azure subscription we can use to explore the Azure portal. We're going to create a free trial account at azure.microsoft.com/free. For verification, we'll need three things, a Microsoft account, and I'll explain that more shortly, you'll need a phone number where a verification code can be sent, and you'll need a credit card. The card won't get charged, not unless you manually upgrade the account to a pay-as-you-go account. If you already have a pay-as-you-go account, you can just use that instead, but you will get charged for everything you create. Let's go to azure.microsoft.com/free.

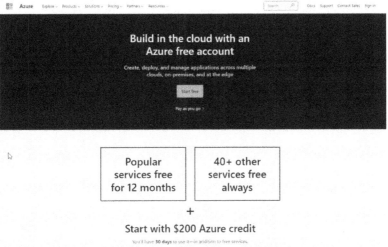

If you've never signed up for a free account, you can do that and get 200 USD credit for 30 days to use for creating resources in Azure. In addition to that, there are certain services that are free for 12 months and other services that are always free, but they're pretty limited in functionality. If we scroll down a bit, this page describes some of the things we can do in Azure, like hosting web applications using Azure App Services, using Azure Machine Learning, creating Azure Virtual Machines or containers, and serverless options like Azure Functions and Azure Logic Apps, which let you build workflows with tons of connectors to services inside and outside of Azure.

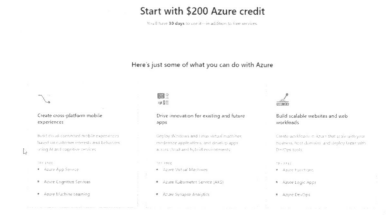

We'll talk about all these services later on. Further down, it says that if we upgrade this free trial to a pay-as-you-go account where our credit card can get billed for usage, we'll be entitled to some free services, like 750 hours of running a Linux or a Windows virtual machine, a 250-GB Azure SQL Database, and 5 GB of blob storage.

We'll talk about storage later on too. But now, let's scroll down and click Start free. The first thing we need is either a Microsoft email address or a GitHub account.

If you're not aware, Microsoft acquired GitHub in 2018, which is why you can use your GitHub identity to create an Azure account. If you're using an email address, it needs to be a Microsoft one, so usually an Outlook, Hotmail or a Live account, but you can even use a phone number now to create a Microsoft account. The point is that you need that Microsoft account already in order to create an Azure account, but you could create the account from this link. I already have a Microsoft account, so I'll enter that email address here and I'll enter my password. I don't have multifactor authentication set up for this Microsoft account, but you could do that in which case you'd need to provide another factor of authentication when logging in, like a code that's generated in the Microsoft Authenticator app on your phone or a temporary code that's sent to you by text or phone call. Now I'm brought to the screen where I can fill in my information. Since I'm logged in, it picks up my name and I need to enter a phone number. This can be a cellphone or a home phone because you can choose to have the code sent to you by text or through an automated voice call. I'll choose Text me and I get a text on my cell phone with a code. So I'll enter that code here and click Verify code. Now I need to enter my address.

Now we need to agree to the customer agreement and privacy agreement. There are links here, of course, so feel free to read through those if you'd like before agreeing. I'll click Next and here's where you need to enter the credit card.

It says you won't be charged unless you move to pay-as-you-go pricing. You should use a credit card here that's never been used for a free trial account, otherwise you may get denied, which makes sense because you shouldn't be able to keep creating free trials in order to get credits to use Azure for free. So I'll enter my credit card info, and just click Sign up. Microsoft will verify your credit card, and once that's done you'll come to a screen that says you're approved and there's a link that will bring you to the Azure portal. So let's go to portal.azure.com, which is the administrative portal for Azure and the browser brings me into the portal.

Next, we'll explore the Azure portal a bit and see how to create a resource in Azure.

Chapter 5 How to Create Resources in Azure

I'm logged into the Azure portal at portal.azure.com. An Azure Active Directory instance gets created with this Azure trial, which means we can create individual users and assign them permissions, so you don't have to keep using this administrative account to log in and really you probably shouldn't because it has superuser privileges. It's a good idea to create an administrative account in Azure AD and use that instead. On this home page, you can access some Azure services, and there's a menu on the left that has shortcuts to some default services, like any Azure virtual machines you've created, SQL databases, and the Azure Active Directory associated with this subscription.

You can access the list of all services from this menu item. You'll see a tour of the Azure portal later, but let's just look at creating a resource. I'll choose the Virtual machines link here.

All services

That brings us to a page where all the virtual machines that were created in this subscription are listed, and of course there aren't any yet.

Let's select the drop-down list to create one, and at this point we haven't selected whether this will be a Linux or a Windows VM. That's fine. What I really want to show you here are some of the mandatory inputs.

The first one is the subscription, and that's filled out automatically. And then there's the resource group that this virtual machine will belong to. Resource groups are basically a container that holds resources, and everything in Azure, including a virtual machine, is considered a resource. We'll talk about how resource groups are used for security and deployment purposes later on. The other thing is the region. You need to select the region that this virtual machine will be created in, which basically means the datacenter where it will exist. The list is pretty small, but that's because we're using a free trial account. Microsoft limits the datacenters available, so regions in high demand don't use too much capacity on free trials. But you could contact Microsoft support if you really want to create this VM in a region that's not listed here. I won't go through anything else on this page. We'll look at creating virtual machines in the next chapter. So, now you know that you'll need to choose a region when creating a resource. Let's talk about regions in Azure in more detail, next.

Chapter 6 What are Azure Regions & Availability Zones

Now let's talk about how Azure is physically implemented. You create services in Azure, like an Azure App Service for hosting a web app or a storage account for storing files. You can then deploy your applications and files to those services. That all gets hosted on Virtual Machines in Azure. Depending on the service you choose, you may have more or less access to those virtual servers for configuration. If you create a virtual machine, for example, you have full control. If you create an app service, you don't have direct access to the virtual machine. But the virtual servers in Azure are hosted on physical servers somewhere. That somewhere is an Azure datacenter. Azure datacenters are physical buildings located all around the world. At the time, there are over 200 Microsoft Azure datacenters worldwide. Each datacenter houses thousands of servers. There are about 4 million physical servers throughout the world. We're going to talk more about how datacenters are implemented later on too. Datacenters are located in regions. A region is a geographic location, often consisting of multiple datacenters. A region is what you choose when you create a resource. You decide which region you want your service created in. We'll talk about considerations in choosing a region in just a little bit. There are often multiple datacenters within a region, which helps in case a single datacenter becomes unavailable. But within certain regions, there's what's called availability zones. Availability zones are unique physical locations within a single region. There's a minimum of three separate availability zones in the region, and each availability zone is made up of one or more datacenters equipped with independent power, cooling, and networking. Some services like zone-redundant storage in Azure storage accounts will replicate your data automatically across all the zones in the region. Every region is located within a geography, which in Azure is a group of regions that define a boundary for data residency and disaster recovery. A geography is generally a single country, but it can be made up of multiple countries. Within a geography, there are region pairs available. Region pairs are datacenters that are generally at least 300 miles apart to reduce the impact on availability caused by a natural disaster or a major power outage. They're connected through a dedicated regional low-latency network. Regional pairs allow you to configure automatic replication and failover for certain Azure services, like when you choose georedundant storage for your Azure storage account. Azure automatically makes copies of your data across the regions in the region pair. For services that don't have built-in options for failover like that, you can design your own strategy for failing over to another region if your primary region isn't available. Virtual machines are an example of this. You have to deploy duplicate virtual machines in another region yourself if you want to have them available for failover. This is called the shared responsibility model in Azure. The services are there for you, you just have to design the solution to take advantage of them. This page in the Azure documentation shows you the regions that are available in the different Azure geographies.

Find the Azure geography that meets your needs

Get all of the information you need to get started on Azure in the geography that best fits your needs, from compliance to resiliency features. Select an Azure geography using the drop-down menu and compare to other geographies nearby.

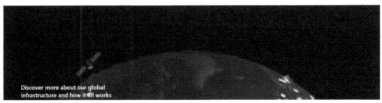

Discover more about our global infrastructure and how it all works

You can see some geographies have more regions than others.

And on this page in the docs, you can see the region pairs that are available.

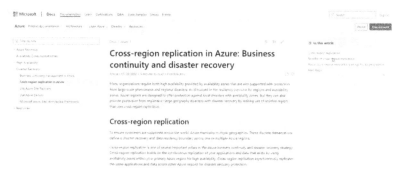

Cross-region replication in Azure: Business continuity and disaster recovery

Many organizations require both high availability provided by availability zones that are also supported with protection from large-scale phenomena and regional disasters. As discussed in the resiliency overview for regions and availability zones, Azure regions are designed to offer protection against local disasters with availability zones, but they can also provide protection from regional or large geography disasters with disaster recovery by making use of another region that uses cross-region replication.

Cross-region replication

To ensure customers are supported across the world, Azure maintains multiple geographies. These discrete demarcations define a disaster recovery and data residency boundary across one or multiple Azure regions.

Cross-region replication is one of several important pillars in the Azure business continuity and disaster recovery strategy. Cross-region replication builds on the synchronous replication of your applications and data that exists by using availability zones within your primary Azure region for high availability. Cross-region replication asynchronously replicates the same applications and data across other Azure regions for disaster recovery protection.

They're generally located in the same country, but not always.

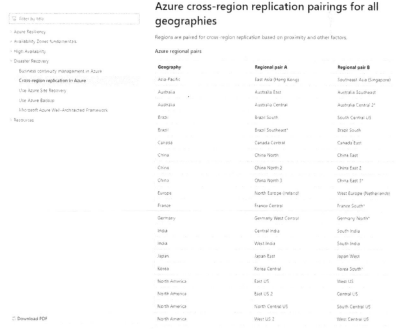

Azure cross-region replication pairings for all geographies

Regions are paired for cross-region replication based on proximity and other factors.

Azure regional pairs

Geography	Regional pair A	Regional pair B
Asia-Pacific	East Asia (Hong Kong)	Southeast Asia (Singapore)
Australia	Australia East	Australia Southeast
Australia	Australia Central	Australia Central 2*
Brazil	Brazil South	South Central US
Brazil	Brazil Southeast*	Brazil South
Canada	Canada Central	Canada East
China	China North	China East
China	China North 2	China East 2
China	China North 3	China East 3*
Europe	North Europe (Ireland)	West Europe (Netherlands)
France	France Central	France South*
Germany	Germany West Central	Germany North*
India	Central India	South India
India	West India	South India
Japan	Japan East	Japan West
Korea	Korea Central	Korea South*
North America	East US	West US
North America	East US 2	Central US
North America	North Central US	South Central US
North America	West US 2	West Central US

For example, at the bottom, it says that the Brazil South region is paired with the South Central US region.

(*) Certain regions are access restricted to support specific customer scenarios, such as in-country disaster recovery. These regions are available only upon request by creating a new support request in the Azure portal (*).

ⓘ Important

- West India is paired in one direction only. West India's secondary region is South India, but South India's
  secondary region is Central India.
- Brazil South is unique because it's paired with a region outside of its geography. Brazil South's secondary
  region is South Central US. The secondary region of South Central US isn't Brazil South.

Next, let's talk about the factors that go into choosing an Azure region to deploy your resources to.

Chapter 7 How to Choose Azure Region for Deploying Resources

Now, let's talk about the factors that go into choosing an Azure region when you're creating resources in Azure. The first is proximity to users, and this has to do with performance. There are physical limitations to how fast data can travel around the world. If most of your users are located in Australia, for example, it doesn't make sense to host your website and database in a datacenter in the United States and have every request and response travel around the world, unless of course there are other reasons to choose that datacenter. One such consideration is that not all Azure services are available in all regions, especially when they're first released. You can go to this page in the Azure docs to see what services are available in which regions.

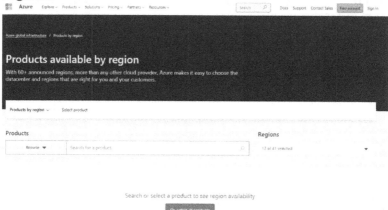

You can choose the regions and the service you're interested in or remove the filter and scroll through all the services to see what's available. Notice how there are services that are nonregional.

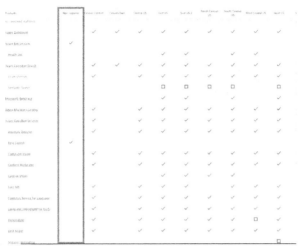

These are ones that don't require you to choose a region when you create them, like the Azure Bot Services. It's also possible that within a specific service, some features might not be available in the region closest to you. A great example of this are different sizes for virtual machines. On the virtual machine pricing page, if I scroll down, the region is selected as East US.

General purpose

Balanced CPU-to-memory ratio. Ideal for testing and development, small to medium databases, and low to medium traffic web servers.

All the classes of VMs are shown below. The amount of cores, RAM, and temporary storage is shown for each.

So, there are basic VMs and there are specialized ones for things like processor-intensive compute tasks. I'll just search for a certain class of VMs. And they're shown here for East US, but if I change the region to South Central US, pricing is not available for this region because you can't create this class of VM there.

So that's a consideration when choosing a region if you have specific needs for certain services. Another reason you might choose one region over another is for regulatory or compliance reasons with regards to data residency. If you work in an industry that's highly regulated or your company has policies around where the data must reside, then you might need to choose your region based on that criteria. Now let's talk about how datacenters are connected together, and for this I want to show you this awesome interactive page on microsoft.com. This lets you choose a geography which tells you how many regions are available, and then you can choose the regions and see details like where it's located, the year it opened, how many availability zones the region has, some of the products available, information on disaster recovery options like region pairing, and standards that the datacenter complies with.

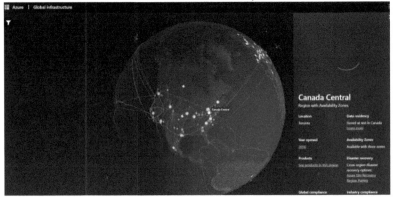

On this map, you can also see how the Microsoft global network is connected. There's over 165,000 miles of fiber optic and undersea cable systems that connect Azure datacenters around the world. When you access a resource in Azure, the traffic goes from your computer through your internet service provider to a point of presence, or PoP, that's managed by Microsoft where it enters into the Microsoft global network. Microsoft has over 185 of these PoPs around the world, so you get routed to the one closest to your location. You can click on these PoPs on the interactive map. PoPs are often placed within milliseconds of global population centers. Then, IP traffic stays on the Microsoft global network to access resources in Azure where it stays encrypted, flowing across the fiber and undersea cables to datacenter regions. You choose which regions to create your Azure resources in, so you can place your applications and data closest to where your users are, which helps keep the response time quick. Next, let's talk about Azure datacenters in more detail.

Chapter 8 Azure Data Centre Fundamentals

A Microsoft datacenter is a physical location that often looks like a bunch of warehouses. You can actually see a tour of a datacenter on microsoft.com. There's a virtual tour version as well that leads you through the areas of a datacenter. Each warehouse is big enough to store a commercial aircraft just to give you a sense of the size. Inside those warehouses are thousands of physical computers that host the virtual servers that you use when you create resources in Azure. The datacenter is built to withstand failures of individual components, so it has redundant networking, electricity, and cooling systems, as well as backup power sources. Because Microsoft hosts so many customers in their datacenters, you get the economy of scale of sharing those resources. Of course, your data is all separate from other customers and encrypted, and Azure datacenters undergo security reviews and have many industry certifications to ensure that your data is protected. Multilayered security is used to protect physical datacenters, infrastructure, and operations, and Microsoft has over 3500 cybersecurity experts monitoring activities in order to protect your business assets and data. So Microsoft is investing a lot more effort in security than any single customer could with their own on-premises datacenters. Microsoft used to be pretty secretive about their datacenters, but now they're more open about how their datacenters are structured and are working to standardize server and datacenter design through the Open Compute Project. Design specifications for server racks and server blades are being shared with the open source community through Project Olympus, similar to how software is made open source. Now let's talk about the energy needed to power a datacenter because this is a major consideration not only affecting cost, but affecting the environment, and that may be important to you when considering using Azure. Microsoft often chooses datacenter locations based on proximity to renewable energy sources. Microsoft enters into agreements with power companies to build wind and solar farms across thousands of acres of land. They build datacenters near hydroelectric dams and choose temperate locations so datacenters can be cooled by the outside air. There's even a project to convert waste heat from new datacenters in Finland into heating for cities. Heat is going to be transferred to customers through a system of insulated pipes for residential and commercial heating requirements. When it comes to backup power systems at datacenters, they are often powered by diesel fuel, but Microsoft is researching alternatives like synthetic fuels and hydrogen fuel cells. They plan to eliminate dependency on diesel by 2030. Let's look at the global infrastructure map again.

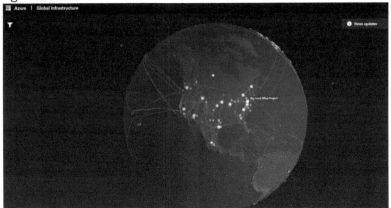

The yellow icons represent renewable energy projects that Microsoft is involved in for wind and solar. These are long-term purchase agreements with third parties. There's a lot of research and innovation going on into datacenter design, and especially cooling. One interesting development is Project Natick, which is an underwater datacenter that was operated for five years off the coast of Scotland where servers were housed in a sealed container at the bottom of the ocean floor. That allowed servers to be cooled using the temperature of the ocean. Another interesting development is the Azure Modular Datacenter. This is a shipping container that allows for setting up an Azure datacenter in a remote area where cloud computing wouldn't have been possible. They use Azure Stack to create a private cloud. These modular datacenters can be used as a mobile command center for humanitarian assistance, for military missions, and to set up wherever high performance computing is needed, and they can run connected to the internet or disconnected. So there's lots of interesting things happening with regards to Microsoft Azure datacenters, and you can read about it for hours online. But the important thing is that Microsoft spends a lot of effort on optimizing the design of their datacenters. Next, let's talk about the resources you create in Azure and how they're logically organized using resources groups

Chapter 9 Resources and Resource Group Basics

Now let's talk about resources and resource groups in Azure. A resource is just a manageable item in Azure. Let's take a look at the Azure portal. The All resources menu item shows all the resources that have been created in this subscription.

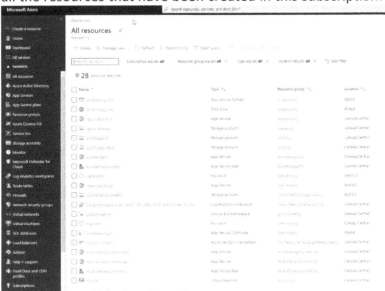

This includes things like App Services for web apps, Storage accounts, there's a Log Analytics workspace where logs are stored from the various services, a Key vault where encryption keys and certificates are securely stored, and there's a Virtual machine here. When you create a virtual machine, other resources are created too, like a public IP address for the VM so it can be reached over the internet, a disk to hold the operating system, a virtual network that the VM is connected to, and a network security group that's used to secure the network. We'll look at all these elements later on, but the point is pretty much anything that can be configured in Azure is considered a resource, even when you

38

think it might just be part of another resource. Each of the resources in this list were created in a location, which is an Azure region, and each resources part of a subscription. A resource group is a container that holds a set of resources that share the same lifecycle. In other words, you deploy, update, and delete them together. You can add and remove individual resources to and from a resource group as your solution evolves, but the general guidance is that if a resource needs to exist on a different deployment cycle, then it should be in another resource group. Each resource you provision can only exist in one resource group. You can move a resource to another resource group if you need to, but it won't exist in both resource groups. Resources in different groups can communicate with each other. For example, you might have three different web applications being maintained by three different teams and they all exist in their own individual resource groups, but they all share a common database. That database can be in a completely different resource group and those web apps will still be able to use it. One of the main features of a resource group is that you can apply security controls to it for administrative actions, so you can assign reader roles to developers to be able to see what resources are in the resource group, but only administrators can make changes to the resource group. Resource groups allow you to leverage Resource Manager templates so you can deploy a set of resources using a JSON template and you can export a template from an existing resource group in order to deploy those resources in a repeatable way. This is great for moving a solution from a dev environment into a production environment, for example. When you create a resource group, you specify a region that it gets created in, but a resource group is just a container with metadata about the resources it contains, so the resource group can be created in a different region than the resources in the group. You can create a resource group during the creation of most resources, like when you're in the process of creating a new virtual machine. In that case, the resource group will get created in the same region that you specify for the virtual machine. You can also create the resource group by itself and then select it as the resource group to use when creating other resources. Next, let's explore the Azure portal, and in the process we'll create a resource group.

Chapter 10 How to Explore Azure Portal

Once you have an Azure account, you have access to the subscriptions associated with that account by going to portal.azure.com. I'll select the Microsoft account I used to create this Azure account. And I supplied my password earlier, so I'm already logged into my Microsoft account in this browser. That brings us into the Azure portal, and by default we're brought to the home page, which has some shortcuts, including shortcuts to create resources in Azure. Let's look at the menu across the top. At the top right is information about your logged-in account. There's a link to sign out, a link to go to the details of this Microsoft account, and the ability to switch directories. We'll talk about Azure Active Directory tenants later on, which is what this refers to. You can also access a link here to be taken to view your Azure bill if you have one.

Next across the top is the ability to send feedback to Microsoft. Then there's a link for Support + troubleshooting. Azure provides unlimited free support for subscription management, and for technical questions there are several support plans available which do have costs involved, but during a trial, you get the Developer support plan for free, which is normally a paid plan. Next is the Portal settings.

The first tab here has to do with directory management, which again involves Azure Active Directory, so I won't talk about that just yet. But this is the one I want to show you, Appearance + startup views.

I personally like to see the left menu permanently docked and also prefer the first screen I see to be the dashboard. Let's apply these changes. Now that menu appears on the left.

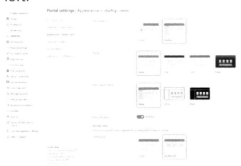

We'll talk about this in a second, but first let's finish off with the menu at the top. The Notifications link shows anything that's in progress or has recently happened, like when you create a resource in Azure it will show here that it's in process and when it's finished being created. The next link is to change directories. So, this is just a shortcut to the first tab on the Portal settings. This farthest link on the left is for the Azure Cloud Shell.

This is basically a command line interface right within the Azure portal that lets you run PowerShell commands and commands for the Azure CLI, or command line interface. Those are powerful ways to manage Azure, and we'll take a look at them later on too, as well as using this Azure Cloud Shell. Now let's look at the menu on the left.

The Home link shows that screen we saw when we first logged into Azure, so that was the home screen. The dashboard is the screen that will get shown from now on when I log in because of the portal settings I changed. The dashboard is a focused view of your resources in Azure. You can visualize data from multiple resources here and pin charts and views to get a complete picture of the health and performance of applications you create in Azure. That'll make more sense as we go along. You can add and manage tiles, and they can be configured individually or you can modify the whole page by adding and removing tiles. There's some suggested ones here, but you can pin pretty much anything in Azure to your dashboard. You can create multiple dashboards, so you can have one for viewing the state of certain applications or one for viewing the state of all the virtual machines, basically whatever you want to see at a glance. Next, let's create a resource group in the Azure portal.

Chapter 11 How to Create Resource Groups in Azure

Since we talked about resource groups earlier, let's look at how to create one in the portal. You can do that from the existing list of resource groups. Along the left here are shortcuts to the various resource types in Azure.

You can modify this to list the types of resources you normally manage, but this is the default. So I don't have any resource groups yet, of course, but from the Create button we can create one. But before we do that, let's pretend we don't have a shortcut on the left menu for this type of resource. In that case, we can go to All services on the menu. From there, we could browse the categories or search for the name of the resource type we want to create or manage. If I click on the resource type, we get brought to the same screen as before. And this little pin beside the name of the resource type, this is how you would pin this view or list to the dashboard. The third way to create a resource is from the link, Create a resource.

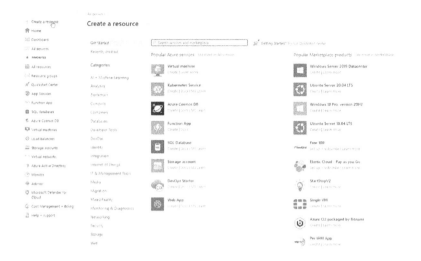

That opens the Azure Marketplace, which Microsoft calls its online store of IT software applications and services built by industry-leading companies. It looks similar to the All services screen you saw with categories of different types of services along the left, and you can use this to create basic Azure services, like a resource group. But the Azure Marketplace also contains add-ons you can install and sometimes purchase from other companies, like SendGrid is listed here, which is an online email service you can set up and use in your solutions. That's not a Microsoft service, so it's available here in the Marketplace, but not on the All services menu. Let's look at some of the categories here. Compute is where Azure services like virtual machines and function apps can be created, but also where preconfigured VMs can be chosen, like certain Linux distributions or a Windows Server VM with Visual Studio already installed. Storage has Azure storage accounts, but also offerings from other vendors that work in Azure on the right side. Same with Web. You can install plain Azure services or install a VM with WordPress already configured and ready to be used.

But let's just search for resource group from here, and it shows up in the results, so let's click this. Now, instead of being brought to the list of resource groups in our subscription, we're brought to the Marketplace view, which provides an overview of the service, information about plans that are available, and so on.

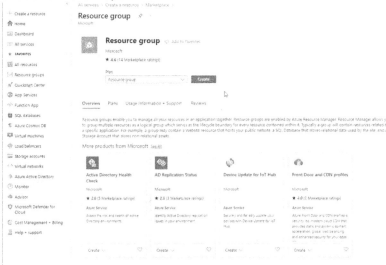

Of course, there's not much here because this is just a basic Azure service, so let's create this resource. We're brought to the create screen and our subscription is selected by default. I'm only logged into one subscription.

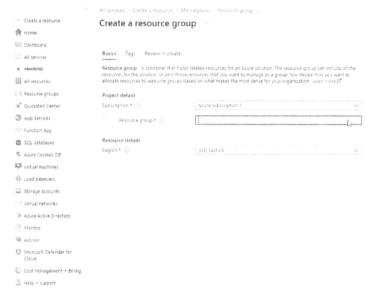

Create a resource group

Basics   Tags   Review + create

Resource group : A container that holds related resources for an Azure solution. The resource group can include all the resources for the solution, or only those resources that you want to manage as a group. You decide how you want to allocate resources to resource groups based on what makes the most sense for your organization. Learn more

Project details

Subscription *

Resource group *

Resource details

Region *

We need to choose a name for this resource group, and this only needs to be unique within our subscription, not across all of Azure. You can name it whatever you want, it's just a string, but often companies come up with a naming convention for sorting and for searching. I like to end my resource names with an abbreviation of the resource type, so in this case I'll add an underscore and rg for resource group. Now you have to choose the region. A resource group is just metadata about all of the resources in the group, so this isn't where those resources will get created. You'll choose that separately for each individual resource that you create. This is just where the resource group or metadata itself will get created. I'll select the Azure region closest to me. Creating a resource in Azure is kind of like a wizard. You move through the tabs using the buttons at the bottom. The next page is Tags. Tags are key value pairs of metadata that you can add to resources, so they can be searched and grouped together.

Create a resource group

Basics   Tags   Review + create

Apply tags to your Azure resources to logically organize them by categories. A tag consists of a key (name) and a value. Tag names are case-insensitive and tag values are case-sensitive. Learn more

Name	Value	Resource
		Resource group

You might use this to mark that a resource belongs to a certain application or a business group or an environment. Tags are helpful when it comes to billing too. There's a service in Azure for cost management, and you can filter resources by tags to see how much all the resources with a particular tag are costing you. You can also download a detailed spreadsheet of costs, and tags are included there for filtering purposes too. I've just added an environment tag. Let's move to the next screen. This is just a summary, so I'll click Create. We can see the new resource group by going to the Resource groups shortcut in the menu. Now we have one item listed.

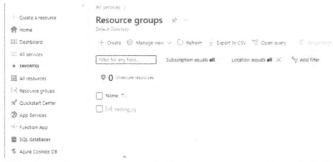

I'll click the name, and that opens up the details for this resource group. The menu items are organized into groups, and this first group is common to all resources in Azure.

The Overview tab is where we can see all the resources included in this resource group. Of course there aren't any yet. We can also delete the resource group from the top menu. The Activity log is where any activity shows. I've already created and deleted a resource group with the exact same name, so it seems to be showing those activities on this resource group. The Access control tab is where you specify who can access the resource and what permissions they have. Of course there's only my account, and I'm the owner so I have full permissions, but you might want to grant someone read-only access so they can't modify resources here. Tags is where we can manage the tags for the resource. The next group of menu items are different depending on the type of resource you create, but you'll often see entries for monitoring metrics and logs for the particular resource. Now let's close out of these and go to All resources. We actually don't have anything here.

Resource groups don't show up in all resources; just resources contained in resource groups are listed here. that's a tour of the Azure portal and resource groups. Next, let's talk about Azure Active Directory.

Chapter 12 Azure Active Directory Basics

You probably don't plan on being the only person managing or using the resources in Azure. So now, let's talk about the directory in your subscription that stores user identities. That's called Azure Active Directory.

I've got a shortcut on the left menu, but let's go to All services, and Azure AD is right here at the top. This is called an Azure Active Directory tenant. When a subscription gets created, it gets its own tenant, so it's a place where the users for your organization only are managed. The Azure AD tenant is the container for users and groups that you want to give access to resources in Azure. That could be to administer things like deploying web apps or creating containers in Azure Blob storage, or it could be user identities for end users for accessing a web application or uploading data to that file storage. On the Users blade, and by the way, when you click a menu option, the panel that opens with the details is called a blade, so this is where all the users in this directory are listed. You can manually add users here, On-premises sync enabled. This means that you can actually synchronize your on-premises Active Directory with this Azure Active Directory tenant and then assign those on-premises users permissions in Azure. You do that by downloading and installing a tool on-premises called Azure AD sync. this identity is a Microsoft account. It has a really long identifier because it's an external entity. I'll show you shortly how you can use your own custom domain name for your company here, but let's create a new user first.

When you create a user, the first option you have is whether you want to create the user identity in this Azure AD tenant or you want to invite an external user. External users are part of something called Azure B2B collaboration, or business to business. That's for users outside your organization who aren't part of an Azure Active Directory tenant, and it lets you give them access to applications and services. They become an object in your Azure Active Directory that you can assign permissions to, but their sign-in process is handled by their own external identity provider. Let's create a generic account called administrator. I'll just give it a name, and we can create the password or let Azure do it. Just make sure you copy this somewhere. You won't see it again, but you can reset it. It says in the Notifications area that the user was created successfully. Let's drill into the details for this user. From here, we can add this user to groups. Groups let you create, well, groups of users, so you can then assign roles to either individual users or to groups.

Those roles are used to provide access to resources in the subscription. You don't have to use groups, but it makes management a lot easier. There are lots of roles in Azure, and they can get pretty granular in terms of what they allow. Let's just give this user the Global administrator role. That will allow them to perform pretty much any action in Azure. So I'll add this role and then refresh the view. It might take a few seconds for the portal to pick up the change. This user has the Global admin role now. Farther down the menu, you can assign licenses.

By default, your Azure AD tenant has the Azure Active Directory Free license, but there are other licenses that you can assign to individual users, like Azure AD Premium P1 or P2 licenses. These give users additional features, like being eligible for Conditional Access policies. I won't go into too much depth on Conditional Access policies, but basically they allow Azure to make authorization decisions based on things like the Azure AD groups that the user belongs to or the location the user is coming from and characteristics about the device they're using. Conditional Access policies can also work with Azure AD Identity Protection, which uses machine learning to identify risky sign-in behavior. If the user is approved to sign in after the Conditional Access policies are evaluated, you can also choose to enforce multi-factor authentication. That's where a user needs to provide a second factor of authentication after their username and password, and that's enabled by a service called Azure Multi-Factor Authentication, which can text a one-time passcode to the user's mobile device that they then enter into the browser to complete their login to applications in Azure. There's also an app the user can install on their device called the Microsoft Authenticator app. Azure can send push notifications to the app for the user to approve a sign in that was initiated in the browser. The app can also generate a rolling token code every 30 seconds that can be used when logging into Azure. That's just a quick introduction to Azure MFA. There's more to it than that, like being able to use the Microsoft Authenticator app for passwordless authentication. Let's go back to the Azure Active Directory tenant that we were looking at. You can use Azure MFA with Conditional Access policies if your users have at least an Azure AD Premium P1 license.

You can also enable it for individual users so they always have to use multi-factor authentication, and you do that from this screen. Let's go back up the hierarchy here to the root of this Azure Active Directory tenant.

Another thing you can create in Azure AD is app registrations, which represent an application, like a mobile app or a web app or a web API. It creates a trust relationship between your app and Azure AD, then those applications can use Azure AD to log in their users. Remember I mentioned that you can sync your on-premises Active Directory with this Azure AD tenant.

That's done using Azure AD Connect, and you can download the tool to install it on-premises from this blade. Then you have options on how to set up that connection, either directly or using federation with a tool like AD FS. I also mentioned earlier that you aren't restricted to the domain name that Azure creates for you.

You can add your company's own domain name to this Azure AD tenant. You need to own that domain name, though, just like you would have to own it when using it for a website. You can purchase a domain name from a domain name registrar. But let's create a new user and let's look at the domain drop-down list in the tenant. It shows both domain names, the default one that Azure created and the one I added, so I can create a user principal name. That's all for Azure Active Directory for now. You might have some questions still about subscriptions and directories and how they relate, so let's talk about that relationship in a little more detail next.

Chapter 13 Azure Directories & Subscriptions

Let's tie together some of the concepts you've learned about so far. Earlier when we created an Azure free trial, we used a Microsoft email account, and that created an Azure account. An Azure account is referred to as a billing account in the documentation. It's an entity that can have subscriptions. In other words, I can create multiple subscriptions and access all of them when I log in with my account. The documentation says there are several types of billing accounts. The Microsoft Online Services Program contains the Azure free account that we created. It also contains the pay-as-you-go accounts that charge our credit card for the resources consumed and the Visual Studio subscriber accounts that are basically pay-as-you-go accounts with some free credits. There are also enterprise agreements for organizations, Microsoft Customer Agreements also for organizations, and Microsoft Partner Agreements for cloud solution providers. Let's look at how these relate to subscriptions. For the type of account we created, we can have multiple subscriptions, so I could continue with my free trial subscription and also create a pay-as-you-go subscription, or I could upgrade the free trial subscription to a pay as you go.

Microsoft Online Services Program

Each of those subscriptions gets an invoice showing the resources that were consumed each month, and each subscription has a payment method, a credit card. Within a subscription, resources are created, and they're actually created within resource groups. We won't look at the other billing account types. They just add some additional layers for management and accounting. When we signed up for the Azure free trial, a subscription was created, and there was an Azure Active directory tenant created too, so you might assume that this is a one-to-one relationship, but it doesn't have to be. Multiple subscriptions can have a trust relationship with the same Azure Active directory tenant, but each subscription can only be linked to one Azure Active Directory tenant, and you can change the tenant that the subscription trusts. To recap, an account can have multiple subscriptions. Subscriptions contain multiple resource groups, and resources groups contain resources. A resource can only belong to a single resource group, and a subscription has a trust relationship with an Azure Active Directory tenant. The subscription trusts Azure Active Directory to authenticate users, services, and devices. You can have multiple subscriptions trust the same Azure AD tenant, but each subscription can only trust a single directory, and all of the users have a single home directory for authentication, but each user can also be a guest in other directories. Okay, so you might be wondering why would you want to have multiple subscriptions? You might want individual subscriptions for different environments like dev and production and be able to apply separate access to manage each subscription using role-based access control, or you might want to keep resources separate in different subscriptions to make billing easier because each subscription can provide a bill for the resources that it uses, so maybe different business groups in your organization want that. Having multiple subscriptions might seem like it could be a management nightmare, but there's something called management groups that make this easier. Management groups can contain multiple subscriptions. They can also contain other management groups so you can create a hierarchy. Maybe you create management groups for different departments so they each have their own subscriptions or for different geo-regions, however your organization is structured. Then you can manage security for your subscriptions at the management group level. Permissions given at the management group level will get inherited by the management groups and subscriptions underneath. All of the subscriptions under the management group need to trust the same Azure Active Directory tenant, though. There's also something in Azure called Policies, and these allow you to set rules, like virtual machines can only get created in the East US region. Then you apply that policy to a subscription or at the management group level and it gets enforced and reported on. We won't get into Azure Policies in this book, but just know that you can use built-in ones, like requiring all resources to use certain tags or more complex policies like ones that enforce compliance to FedRAMP and HIPAA standards. You can browse all the built-in policies available in Azure on docs.microsoft.com, and you can also create your own custom policies and apply them to your management groups and subscriptions. In summary, so far you have learned how instances of services that you create are organized into subscriptions and resource groups, and you learned how the underlying physical Azure platform is implemented through regions and datacenters. You also saw how to create an Azure subscription, navigate the portal, and create resources, and you learned about how Azure Active Directory is used to manage identity and access for managing Azure, as well as being used as the foundation for access control by users of your applications. Next, we're going to look at some of the services in Azure used for compute, like virtual machines and app services.

Chapter 14 Azure Service Models

Let's talk about cloud computing service models. This might be a review for you, but it helps to put Azure compute options into perspective. These are categories that describe how much a resource is managed for you in the cloud. Another way to look at it is how much responsibility do you have with regards to managing the resource. Let's look at each of these. The on-premises model isn't a cloud model at all, it's just here to explain all the things that you're responsible for when you host your own infrastructure on-premises. This is what we talked about earlier, but besides all the physical infrastructure, if you're hosting your applications on virtual servers, then there's virtualization software that needs to be configured and managed. Then you're responsible to configure the virtual machines, which includes OS licensing and patching. You're responsible for installing the middleware on the servers and any runtimes, like the .NET Framework or Java, and then managing the data and applications that you host on those virtual servers. When you move to the cloud with the Infrastructure as a Service cloud service model, you can choose to provision resources like virtual servers. In Azure, you can create Windows or Linux VMs and everything below the OS layer of the VM is managed for you, so you don't have to worry about hardware refreshes or disks failing, you just choose the type of virtual machine you want and you pay for it. The cost includes the operating system license, but you can also leverage existing Windows Server licenses you might already own on-premises. You can install whatever you want on the VMs that you provision as Azure Virtual Machines. If you want to install a SQL Server database, for example, you can do that yourself. We'll look at some other options for SQL Server and Azure later on too. The next service model is Platform as a Service, or PaaS. Platform as a Service is a complete development and deployment environment in the cloud. Azure App Service is a compute service in Azure that allows you to host web applications and APIs in a preconfigured environment where all the runtimes are installed, like .NET Core,

Java or PHP. And those frameworks get updated along with the underlying virtual machines that they run on. You only need to manage the applications and services that you develop. Microsoft manages everything else. The third cloud service model is Software as a Service. This is actually the most popular use of cloud computing in terms of the number of users. These are fully functional cloud-based apps that users can connect to over the internet. Office 365 is the Microsoft solution for email, calendars, and office tools. Instead of buying software to install on the desktop and managing your own email servers, you can purchase Office 365 on a pay-as-you-go basis. You can still download and install Office tools like Word and Outlook, but they're also available in the browser. The central hosting of the Exchange Server is handled in the cloud and hosted by Microsoft. SharePoint is another Microsoft offering that falls under Software as a Service. As you can see with the Software as a Service model, you just use the software and you get a fully managed service that's available across devices and platforms. The services you'll be learning about throughout this book fall into the Infrastructure as a Service and Platform as a Service models. Now that you understand a bit about responsibilities with these service models, let's talk more about compute options in Azure next. Then we'll look at the major compute models individually, starting with virtual machines. Next, we'll talk about containers, which allow you to package applications and dependencies for deployment. After that, we'll look at Azure App Service. And finally, explore Azure Functions, which allow you to run small pieces of code without requiring a full-blown application.

Chapter 15 Azure Compute Options

Azure compute is really an overarching category for a bunch of services in Azure that provide on-demand computing power for running cloud-based applications. The main services in Azure compute are virtual machines, container instances, and there are a number of ways to host containers in Azure, Azure App Service and Azure Functions. Let's discuss each of these at a high level and then we'll get into more detail. Virtual machines are software emulations of physical computers. They run on physical computers in Azure, but multiple virtual machines, or VMs, can run on the same physical host and use the resources of that host. You connect to a virtual machine in Azure using a remote desktop client, and you can manage all aspects of the operating system, including installing whatever software on the VM that you want. It gives you the most control, but also requires the most management because you're responsible for all the configuration and security patches and updates required by the operating system on that virtual machine. But you'll see that Azure offers some services to make that easier. Let's talk about some of the benefits of choosing virtual machines in Azure. Virtual machines are probably the most familiar option for most IT pros because they're just like virtual servers that you would maintain on-premises. If you're planning on migrating to Azure from on-premises, virtual machines can provide a lift-and-shift approach by creating VMs in Azure similar to the physical or virtual servers you have on-premises. You might have applications that require operating system resources like registry access or that use authentication mechanisms like Windows Integrated Authentication and you don't want to rewrite those apps to run on cloud services like Azure App Service, or you might have older applications or custom off-the-shelf software that needs to be installed, VMs are the way to go. Besides having the ability to install whatever third-party software you want on the virtual machine, you can deploy your own applications and you can host multiple applications on the VM. So, virtual machines can have some cost savings versus deploying those apps to single instances of other services, but the applications share the resources on the VM, so you need to be aware of one application using too much CPU or memory and affecting the others. Or if multiple applications use a shared library, for example, updating that library to benefit one app could cause another app to break. That's an issue that containers are meant to solve. Containers are used to wrap up an application into its own isolated package. It's for server-based applications and services, so web apps are a typical example. When an app is deployed using a container, everything the application needs to run successfully is included in the container, like runtimes and library dependencies. This makes it easier to move the container around. Containers reduce problems with deploying applications. Containers are kind of like virtual machines, but they run on top of virtual or physical servers using a container runtime layer, similar to how virtual machines run on a virtualization layer. You can host multiple containers on a single virtual machine if you install a container runtime, and Docker is an example of one of those. In terms of the service models we discussed earlier, there are services in Azure that host containers on Platform as a Service offerings, like Azure Container Instances and Container Apps. The next Azure compute services fall under the Platform as a Service model. Azure App Service lets you quickly build and deploy web apps, mobile apps, and API apps that can be leveraged by other applications or accessed by client apps over HTTP using REST. They also allow you to run server-side apps and scripts, similar to how you would install a Windows service on your web servers to perform some task on a timer. You can choose your application runtime, like .NET, Node.js, and several others, and you can choose whether you want the underlying VMs to be Linux or Windows-based. Azure App Services takes care of managing those underlying VMs for you, which is the most obvious benefit, but you also get extra features like built-in integration with authentication providers like Azure Active Directory to handle authenticating users to your applications. You get something called deployment slots, so you can have multiple versions of your app for development and production and quickly swap those deployment slots to promote the apps. App Services also has built-in features to scale out the underlying VMs. You can add and remove virtual machines manually or Azure can autoscale the VMs based on metrics that you configure, like the amount of CPU being used. Azure App Services are great for running web apps and APIs that are used by mobile apps and client apps and other services, but sometimes you just need a piece of code to run in order to do some task like process a file or update a database table or send a message to another service, and that's what Azure Functions are for. It's a service to host small pieces of code, but you can chain functions together or use them as part of other solutions. Functions can run on a timer or in response to events like an HTTP call, and there are built-in triggers that you can use, like if a file changes in Azure Storage that can trigger an Azure Function to run. You only pay for the compute power that you use. For small tasks, Azure Functions are a great way to save effort and money. Azure Functions are often called serverless computing, although that's kind of a loose term. There are always servers involved, it's just how much you need to interact with them. There's another service in Azure that's often categorized as serverless compute also. It's called Azure Logic Apps. These allow you to configure workflows right in the browser and connect to various services inside and outside of Azure using built-in connectors. Logic Apps sometimes get discussed in the context of Azure compute, so we'll look at them later when we discuss Azure Functions. But next, let's look more closely at virtual machines in Azure.

Chapter 16 Azure Virtual Machine Basics

Using Azure Virtual Machines, you can set up servers in the cloud. You can basically recreate your on-premises environment in Azure if you choose. You could have an Active Directory server storing user accounts, a DNS server, web servers, file servers, and database servers. Using a virtual network in Azure, these VMs can all communicate and security can be enabled to restrict ports, all the same things as on-premises except they're in the cloud, so you can also enable access to the internet if you choose. There are additional features of Azure networking like load balancers and firewalls that allow you to secure your VM network. You can also extend your on-premises environment into the cloud by connecting your on-premises network to a VNet in Azure, then the VMs in Azure can essentially become part of your network. So if you're running out of capacity on-premises and don't want to buy new hardware, this is an option. There are several ways to deploy VMs to Azure. You can upload your own VM images into a storage account in Azure and use them as image templates to create instances of virtual machines. There are some steps involved to prepare your disk files, but there's a much easier way to create VMs in Azure by choosing from preconfigured VM images from the Azure Marketplace. Many of them are provided by Microsoft, but also by other third parties. When you create a VM from the Marketplace, the licensing costs for the operating system are included in the price. When you create a virtual machine in Azure, there are a lot of configuration options, but the three big decisions are the image you want to use, the size of the VM, and the availability options. You start by choosing a VM image.

This is the configuration that decides what operating system is installed, and there are several available, like different versions of Windows Server and Windows desktop operating systems or different distributions of Linux. You can also choose images that are preconfigured with software. So you can create a VM image that has WordPress Server already installed or an SMTP server or development tools like Visual Studio. When you create a VM, you also choose the VM size.

Azure has predefined configurations that decide how many virtual CPUs are included and the amount of RAM. Different VM sizes are suitable for different workloads. By browsing the VM pricing page, you can see a description of each size of VM, and they're grouped into categories, series, and then the actual VM instance code that you choose when you create a VM. Under General purpose VMs are the B-series VMs.

General purpose

Balanced CPU-to-memory ratio. Ideal for testing and development, small to medium databases, and low to medium traffic web servers.

Bs-series

Bs-series are economical virtual machines that provide a low-cost option for workloads that typically run at a low to moderate baseline CPU performance, but sometimes need burst to significantly higher CPU performance when the demand rises. These workloads don't require the use of the full CPU all the time, but occasionally will need to burst to some tasks more quickly. Many applications such as development and test servers, low traffic web servers, small databases, micro services, servers for proof-of-concepts, build servers, and code repositories fit into this model.

Instance	Core(s)	RAM	Temporary storage	Pay as you go with AHB	1 year reserved with AHB	3 year reserved with AHB	Spot with AHB	Add to estimate
B1s	1	1 GiB	4 GiB	$7.5920/month	$4.4165/month –41% savings	$2.8616/month –62% savings	- -	[+]
B1ms	1	2 GiB	4 GiB	$15.1110/month	$8.9133/month –41% savings	$5.7232/month –62% savings	- -	[+]
B2s	2	4 GiB	8 GiB	$30.3680/month	$17.7536/month –41% savings	$11.4172/month –62% savings	- -	[+]

It says here these are suitable for development workloads and low traffic web applications and small databases. Farther down, the D2-series VMs are for most production workloads. Within each series, you can choose an instance size with a specific configuration that you need.

D2as – D96as v5 (latest generation without local temporary storage)

The Das-v5-series virtual machines are based on the 3rd Generation AMD EPYC™ 7763v (Milan) processor. This processor's frequency can achieve up to 3.5GHz. The Das v5 VM offer a combination of vCPUs and memory able to meet the requirements associated with most production workloads.

The Das v5 virtual machine sizes do not have any temporary storage thus lowering the price of entry. You can attach Standard SSDs, Standard HDDs, and Premium SSDs disk to these VMs. You can also attach Ultra Disk storage based on its regional availability. Disk storage is billed separately from virtual machines. See pricing for disks.

Instance	vCPU(s)	RAM	Temporary storage	Pay as you go with AHB	1 year reserved with AHB	3 year reserved with AHB	Spot with AHB	Add to estimat
D2as v5	2	8 GiB	0 GiB	$62.7800/month	$36.9964/month ~41% savings	$23.8637/month ~61% savings	$6.9124/month ~88% savings	+
D4as v5	4	16 GiB	0 GiB	$125.5600/month	$74.0804/month ~41% savings	$47.7201/month ~61% savings	$13.8240/month ~83% savings	+
D8as v5	8	32 GiB	0 GiB	$251.1200/month	$148.1681/month ~40% savings	$95.4183/month ~62% savings	$27.6480/month ~88% savings	+
D16as v5	16	64 GiB	0 GiB	$502.2400/month	$296.3362/month ~40% savings	$190.8585/month ~61% savings	$55.2968/month ~88% savings	+

Each size has a pay-as-you-go price and the price is listed per month, but you're actually charged at an hourly rate and you can deallocate a VM when it's not in use to save on compute charges. There are also options with some VM classes to reserve the VM for one or three years. If you expect to be using it for that long, you can get some significant cost savings with that commitment. There's also Spot VMs that allow you to use VMs that come from unused capacity in Azure. You can get them significantly cheaper, but you have to be able to tolerate Azure evicting the VM with only 30 seconds notice so Azure can recover the capacity. If you're just running a DevTest environment or a batch processing job, that might be fine. As you go farther down, the VM series gets more and more specialized.

Compute optimized

High CPU-to-memory ratio. Good for medium traffic web servers, network appliances, batch processes, and application servers.

Fsv2-series

The Fsv2-series virtual machines provide 2 GiB of RAM and 8 GB of local temporary storage (SSD) per vCPU(s) and are optimized for compute-intensive workloads. These VMs are hyper-threaded and based on the Intel® Xeon® Platinum 8272CL (second generation Intel® Xeon® Scalable processors) or the Intel Xeon® Platinum 8168 (Skylake) processors. These virtual machines are ideal for scenarios like batch processing, web servers, analytics, and gaming. The Fsv2 VMs can be attached to Premium SSD or Ultra Disk persistent storage. Persistent storage disks are billed separately from virtual machines. See section for disks.

Instance	vCPU(s)	RAM	Temporary storage	Pay as you go with AHB	1 year reserved with AHB	3 year reserved with AHB	Spot with AHB	Add to estimate
F2s v2	2	4 GiB	16 GiB	$61.7580/month	$36.5000/month ~40% savmgs	$22.6373/month ~63% savmgr	$8.4425/month ~80% savings	+
F4s v2	4	8 GiB	32 GiB	$123.3700/month	$73.0000/month ~40% savings	$45.2527/month ~63% savings	$16.8645/month ~80% savings	+

There are compute optimized servers, which have a high CPU-to-memory ratio.

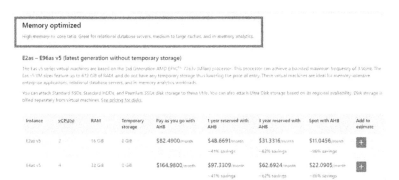

Memory optimized

High memory-to-core ratio. Great for relational database servers, medium to large caches, and in-memory analytics.

E2as – E96as v5 (latest generation without temporary storage)

The Eas v5 series virtual machines are based on the 3rd Generation AMD EPYC™ 7763v (Milan) processor. This processor can achieve a boosted maximum frequency of 3.5GHz. The Eas v5 VM sizes feature up to 672 GiB of RAM, and do not have any temporary storage thus lowering the price of entry. These virtual machines are ideal for memory-intensive enterprise applications, relational database servers, and in-memory analytics workloads.

You can attach Standard SSDs, Standard HDDs, and Premium SSDs disk storage to these VMs. You can also attach Ultra Disk storage based on its regional availability. Disk storage is billed separately from virtual machines. See pricing for disks.

Instance	vCPU(s)	RAM	Temporary storage	Pay as you go with AHB	1 year reserved with AHB	3 year reserved with AHB	Spot with AHB	Add to estimate
E2as v5	2	16 GiB	0 GiB	$82.4900/month	$48.6691/month ~41% savings	$31.3316/month ~62% savings	$11.0456/month ~86% savings	+
E4as v5	4	32 GiB	0 GiB	$164.9800/month	$97.3309/month ~41% savings	$62.6924/month ~62% savings	$22.0905/month ~86% savings	+

Memory-optimized series VMs have higher memory-to-CPU core ratio, so they're better for hosting database servers. You'll notice that some of the series aren't available in the region that's selected above. VMs get more specialized as we go farther down.

HBv3-series Constrained vCPUs capable

HBv3-series VMs are optimized for HPC applications such as fluid dynamics, finite element analysis, financial calculations, weather simulation, molecular dynamics, and silicon RTL.

630 GB/sec of effective memory bandwidth, up to 96 MB of L3 cache per core (1.5 GB per VM), up to 7 GB/s of block device SSD performance, and clock frequencies up to 3.5 GHz. All HBv3-series VMs feature 200 Gb/sec HDR InfiniBand from NVIDIA Networking to enable supercomputer-scale MPI workloads.

Instance	Active vCPU(s) / Underlying vCPU(s)	RAM	Temporary storage	Pay as you go with AHB	1 year reserved with AHB	3 year reserved with AHB	Spot with AHB	5 year reserved with AHB	Add to estimate
HB120-14rs v3	16 / 120	448 GiB	2,100 GiB	$2,628.0000/month	$1,971.0000/month ~24% savings	$1,314.0000/month ~50% savings	$672.7680/month ~74% savings	$875.9197/month ~66% savings	+
HB120-32rs v3	32 / 120	448 GiB	2,100 GiB	$2,628.0000/month	$1,971.0000/month ~24% savings	$1,314.0000/month ~50% savings	$672.7680/month ~74% savings	$875.9197/month ~66% savings	+
HB120-64rs v3	64 / 120	448 GiB	2,100 GiB	$2,628.0000/month	$1,971.0000/month ~24% savings	$1,314.0000/month ~50% savings	$672.7680/month ~74% savings	$875.9197/month ~66% savings	+

It says these HBv3 VMs are optimized for high-performance computing, like financial calculations and weather simulation. That's pretty specific and pretty expensive. There's a new tool in Azure that can make finding the right VM size much easier than reading through all these descriptions.

Virtual machines selector
Find the right VMs for your needs and budget

Ready when you are—let's find your VMs

Find VMs by workload type	Find VMs by OS and software	Find VMs by deployment region
Select your workload and requirements	Select the operating system and software that you'd like to run on the VM	Select the region where you'd like to deploy the VM
Start here >	Start here >	Start here

Help us make this tool better. Did this tool help you find what you're looking for?
If no, tell us what you were looking for.

The virtual machine selector lets you find VM sizes by workload type, OS and software or by deployment region. I won't go through all the screens, but you can select things like the type of operating system and the minimum and maximum number of CPUs and RAM, and it'll produce a list for you. You select a VM size when you create the VM, but it is possible to resize the VM later. That's called scaling up if you're choosing a VM size with more CPU or RAM, or scaling down if you change to a smaller VM size. That's part of the elasticity in the cloud that we talked about previously. You don't have to create a new VM if you need extra processing power, and you can release those resources when you're done with them. Let's talk about the related resources that a VM needs. A virtual machine needs a disk to store the operating system. That's created when you create the VM, and it gets managed by Azure in Azure Storage. It's basically your copy of the VM image. You can also add data disks if you need to store a lot of data as part of your VM. Maybe you need database storage or some other file storage attached to your VM. A VM also needs to exist on a virtual network in Azure, generally referred to as a VNet. That's how it can communicate with other VMs and out to the internet. So even if you only have a single VM, it needs an Azure

Virtual Network. You can either create one while creating the VM or you can attach a VM to an existing virtual network. The VM needs a network interface in order to communicate on the network, and you can have a public IP address for the VM so it can be remotely accessed. That could allow you to use the VM as a web server. You can also set up security rules to filter network traffic between resources on the virtual network using network security groups. We'll talk more about networking in the next module. So each of these is considered a resource in Azure with their own configuration screens, and when you add managed data disks, those have associated costs. Accessing those managed disks also have costs as storage transactions, and any data that comes out of Azure is also charged. That's actually true of Azure in general. It's free to put data into Azure, but there are egress charges when data comes out, like if you're using your VM as a web server, the data in the responses incurs charges. But these are very, very small charges, just something to be aware of when you're pricing out a solution that involves virtual machines. You can estimate your costs in Azure using the Azure pricing calculator. When you add a VM, it will add the related resources that can incur charges. Some related resources, like virtual networks, are actually free. Next, let's talk about the availability options with virtual machines in Azure.

Chapter 17 Azure VM Scale & Availability Sets

By now, you understand that Azure Virtual Machines are hosted on physical machines in an Azure datacenter. Sometimes those physical machines need maintenance or something fails or they need to be restarted. That's just reality. So if you design your solution with a single VM, you're introducing a single point of failure into your application. For that reason, a datacenter is organized into update domains and fault domains, and you can take advantage of these to create a highly available solution using multiple virtual machines. Update domains are groups of virtual machines and the underlying physical hardware that can be rebooted at the same time. Fault domains define a group of virtual machines that share a common power source in the datacenter and a common network switch. When you're creating a virtual machine in Azure, you can choose to create it in an availability set with other VMs. When you do that, Azure places your VMs in separate update domains and fault domains. So you're essentially telling Azure that these VMs are part of an application so Azure can help with the resiliency and availability. This doesn't protect you from things like operating system or application-specific failures, but it does limit the impact of potential hardware failures, network outages, and power interruptions. And you actually need to create at least two VMs within an availability set if you want the 99.95% uptime guarantee in the Azure service-level agreement. To use these VMs for redundancy in a solution, you'd need to put them behind a load balancer. Users access a web server from a single IP address and URL, but the load balancer routes the traffic to one of the VMs in the solution based on availability and load. To make that easier, though, Azure offers something called virtual machine scale sets. These let you create and manage a group of identical virtual machines, and Azure will put them behind a load balancer for you. You can configure virtual machine scale sets to scale with demand so Azure can add and remove VMs from the scale set as needed, and of course you configure the parameters around that. Those VMs are spread across fault domains, so you have that protection as well. Virtual machine scale sets let you maintain a consistent configuration across your VMs. You get resiliency if one of the VMs has a problem, and the autoscaling feature helps with application performance. If you plan to set up a large-scale solution that requires a lot of VMs working together, up to 1000 VMs are supported in a virtual machine scale set.

Chapter 18 How to Create a Virtual Machine in Azure

We could start from the shortcut on the left menu, but let's go to All services and search for virtual machines. I'll click that in the search results, and let's create a VM from the Create button at the top. There's a few options here.

Azure virtual machine with preset configuration just narrows down the VM sizes based on whether you intend this VM for development or production. Azure Arc lets you manage VMs in environments outside Azure, including your on-premises environment. And Azure VMware Solution virtual machine lets you move VMware-based workloads from your datacenter to Azure. Let's just create a VM in Azure. That brings us to the create screen with all the tabs across the top. We'll go in order here.

Create a virtual machine

I won't go through every option on these screens, just some key ones. We need to put this VM in a resource group, and all the related resources will get created there too. We could use the existing resource group, but let's just create a new one. That'll make it easier to delete these resources later. I'll give this new resource group a name. Now I have to give the VM a name. This can be pretty much anything, but you'll probably develop a naming convention for your organization. Next we choose a region. There are only a few regions available because this is a free Azure trial subscription. In a pay-as-you-go subscription, the list is much bigger. Next we choose the availability option. We can choose to use availability zones. This relates back to the discussion on Azure regions.

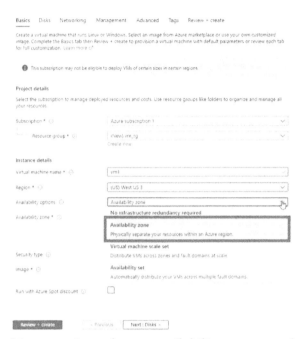

Create a virtual machine

Basics   Disks   Networking   Management   Advanced   Tags   Review + create

Create a virtual machine that runs Linux or Windows. Select an image from Azure marketplace or use your own customized image. Complete the Basics tab then Review + create to provision a virtual machine with default parameters or review each tab for full customization. Learn more

ℹ This subscription may not be eligible to deploy VMs of certain sizes in certain regions.

Project details

Select the subscription to manage deployed resources and costs. Use resource groups like folders to organize and manage all your resources.

Subscription * ⓘ	Azure subscription 1
Resource group * ⓘ	(New) vm_rg
	Create new

Instance details

Virtual machine name * ⓘ	vm1
Region * ⓘ	(US) West US 3
Availability options ⓘ	Availability zone
Availability zone * ⓘ	No infrastructure redundancy required
	Availability zone Physically separate your resources within an Azure region.
	Virtual machine scale set Distribute VMs across zones and fault domains at scale
Security type ⓘ	
Image * ⓘ	Availability set Automatically distribute your VMs across multiple fault domains.
Run with Azure Spot discount ⓘ	☐

Review + create   ← Previous   Next : Disks →

Most regions have availability zones where there are separate datacenters in the region. If you're planning on creating multiple VMs for your solution, you can choose which zone to put the VM in. There are also virtual machine scale sets available and availability sets. Let's choose Availability set. And since there isn't an existing one to add this VM to, I'll create a new one. We can configure the number of fault domains and update domains. Let's just leave the defaults and click OK. Next we choose the image we want to use to create this VM. We can choose from various flavors of Linux or versions of Windows.

Create a virtual machine

I'll just choose a Windows Server image. Next we choose the size. There are a few popular sizes listed here, and we can browse all the sizes and their specs if we want to.

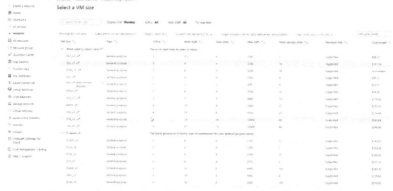

But let's choose the smallest D-series VM listed here. Next we need an administrator name. This will be a local account on this VM. We can add other accounts for access later.

After that, we can open some inbound ports. You'll want at least RDP enabled on a Windows VM so we can remote into it. So I'll leave port 3389, the default RDP port.

Next let's go to Disks.

We can choose the type of disk to use for the operating system, and we can add data disks here, but we can also do that after the VM is created. So let's move on to Networking.

Create a virtual machine

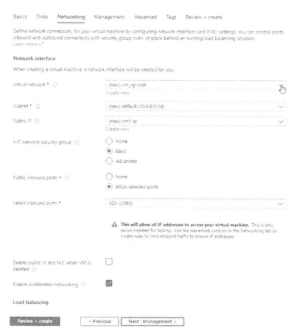

This is where we can add this VM to an existing virtual network or create a new one. Since we don't have an existing VNet, we'll create one. And you can break that VNet into subnets, and then you can place VMs in different subnets and control communication between them. Let's leave the defaults. And the public IP address will get created too. The security on this VNet will be configured to allow access from port 3389 the internet so we can remote in.

We could configure load balancing here if we intend to have multiple VMs as part of this solution.

Let's go to Management. Here we can configure options like boot diagnostics, which lets you debug problems booting up your virtual machine.

You can also create a system-managed identity, which is an Azure AD-managed service account for this VM. So you can do things like grant this VM's service account access to a database or to a storage account in Azure. You can enable auto shutdown. Shutting down a VM in Azure will save you money on compute charges, but you still pay for the storage of the underlying VM. So if this is a VM for development, let's say, you might only need it running during business hours. You can also shut down a VM yourself anytime you want. Let's go to Advanced, and this is where we can configure applications to install after deployment and run custom scripts while the VM is being provisioned.

And we talked about tags earlier, which help with managing large numbers of VMs. Let's review this configuration and create this VM.

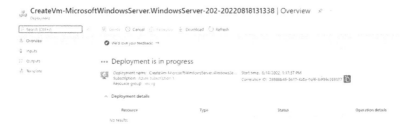

Next, we'll explore the management options once the VM is created.

It took about 2 minutes for everything to get created.

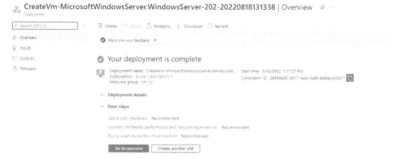

We could go to the VM configuration screen from here, but let's go to All resource groups and let's see the resource group that was created.

You can see all the related resources that were created with the VM itself, like the virtual network, the operating system disk, the network interface, public IP address, and even the availability set is created as a separate resource with its own configuration. Let's drill into the VM. On the Overview tab, you can see the public IP address for this VM. So this is how you would access it from the internet. There's also the private IP address, which is the IP address of the VM on the VNet that was created. And on the Overview tab, you can also stop the VM, and this is how you can save on compute charges when not using the virtual machine.

This releases the server resources associated with the VM, like the underlying CPU and RAM. The Networking tab allows us to manage the ports that are open. We could open up port 80 for HTTP traffic here, for example.

Disks are where you can attach data disks if you need more storage later.

On the Size tab, you can resize the VM. So we could scale it up if we found that the workloads that we're putting on here are more than the VM can handle.

You just choose the new size and click Resize. If the VM is running, this will cause it to restart. On the Configuration tab, you can manage settings like the licensing for the Windows operating system. You might have existing Windows Server licenses you'd like to use in order to save on Azure   costs.

Identity is where you enable the managed identity we discussed during the VM creation screens, and that allows you to provide access to other Azure resources using the Azure Active Directory identity of this VM. Backup is where you can configure options for backing up this VM. Azure has a service called Azure Backup where you can store backups of VM disks, file shares, and blobs in Azure storage. And even databases running on Azure VMs can be backed up. Of course, there are additional costs associated with storing backups. Azure Site Recovery provides disaster recovery by replicating a VM to a different Azure region.

You can use this service to fail over your Azure VMs to another region and also to replicate VMs from other environments for failover to Azure, like on-premises VMs and even Windows virtual machines in Amazon Web Services. The Updates tab lets you use other services in Azure to help you provide updates to this VM.

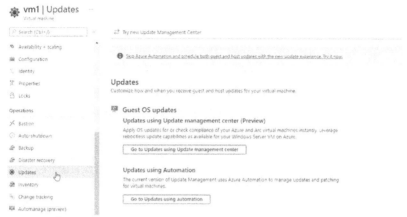

With Infrastructure as a Service VMs, you're responsible for updating them. Azure does help with this, though, by allowing you to leverage a service called Azure Automation to push out updates to VMs that are enrolled with the service. You need to configure that and schedule the updates, though. This works for Windows and Linux VMs. Now let's see how to connect to this VM remotely.

On the connect page, you can connect using Remote Desktop Protocol, SSH or using a service called Azure Bastion, which lets you connect using your browser and the Azure portal. RDP is the traditional way to log into a Windows VM, so let's choose this. Azure is going to create a file for us to download. I'll go to my Downloads folder and let's edit this file. If you've used Remote Desktop Connection before, you see this is just a standard file with the IP address of the VM and the RDP port 3389 already configured. The only account that has access to this VM right now is the local administrator account we created on the VM, so I'll use a different account, and the name is the VM name, backslash, the account name, and the password I used during the VM creation. Once it connects, we're brought into the remote session. Server Manager opens on the VM, and here we can manage the VM and even add it to a domain.

I've used Azure VMs many times to create test environments in the cloud by creating a VM and installing Active Directory and then joining VMs to the network, just like you would on-premises. That's a standalone environment. If you want to give Azure AD users access to this VM and the applications on it, there's a way to do that using Azure AD Domain Services.

Chapter 20 Azure AD Domain Services

First of all, Azure Active Directory is not the same thing as Active Directory on-premises. They both store user identities and allow you to create groups of users for security purposes, but Azure AD was built for the cloud and it uses web authentication protocols for authenticating users like OAuth 2.0 and OpenID Connect. Cloud native services like Azure App Service use these protocols by default. The authentication technologies used most often in on-premises Active Directory is Windows Integrated Authentication, which uses Kerberos and NTLM protocols. With Windows Integrated Authentication, a user logs into the local network and a security token gets passed around so they can get authenticated by any computer that's joined to the network, including web servers. That functionality is provided by domain services, which is just a part of Active Directory. Many legacy applications use Windows Integrated Authentication, so if you're moving them to VMs in Azure, that can be a showstopper. You may not want to modify those applications to use another authentication method, or in the case of commercial off-the-shelf software, you probably can't change the authentication methods that they use. One possible solution if you have an on-premises Active Directory infrastructure is to extend your on-premises network to the cloud and use your Active Directory Domain Services, at least for users in your on-premises Active Directory. You would join the VMs in Azure to the same network as on-premises, so really there's no connection to Azure AD for those servers. For on-premises users accessing applications on the VMs, though, they could still authenticate with Windows Integrated Authentication. But user identities stored only in the cloud have no connection, and you may be looking to minimize your dependency to on-premises AD or you don't plan on having a hybrid cloud at all. So there is a solution in Azure AD, and it's called Azure Active Directory Domain Services. It's not enabled by default, you need to turn it on, and it provides the ability to join virtual machines to managed domain where the user identities are stored in Azure AD, but the VMs can use legacy authentication methods like Kerberos and NTLM. When you set up Azure Active Directory Domain Services, Azure deploys two domain controllers into your selected Azure region, and you don't need to manage or update them. It's handled for you. Information from Azure AD is synchronized into Azure AD Domain Services. Then, applications, services, and virtual machines connected to the managed domain can use common AD features like Domain Join, Group Policy, LDAP, Kerberos, and NTLM authentication. If you have on-premises Active Directory, you learned that you can synchronize users and groups from your on-premises Active Directory to Azure Active Directory. That's not the same thing as joining the two networks. They're still separate, there's just an agent installed in your environment that synchronizes the user accounts into Azure Active Directory on a continuous basis. Then those users can be granted access to applications in Azure. Even though they're accessing the application from on-premises, it's their Azure AD identities that are used. They can still access applications hosted on those virtual machines that use legacy authentication protocols. Before we leave the discussion of virtual machines, let's talk about Azure Virtual Desktop, next.

Chapter 21 Azure Virtual Desktop Basics

Azure Virtual Desktop is a desktop and app virtualization service in Azure. It was previously called Windows Virtual Desktop. Azure Virtual Desktop is used to provide Windows desktops to users with computers actually running in Azure. The user logs into a computer in Azure where all their applications are installed and all their data is accessible, but none of it is stored on their local computer and all the processing by the applications is being done in the cloud. Users can access their remote desktop and applications from any device. There are native apps provided for Windows, Mac, iOS, Android, and an HTML5 interface is also provided, so the remote desktop can be accessed using a web browser too. What's the purpose of Azure Virtual Desktop? What problems does it solve? It separates operating systems, data, and apps from local hardware. That enables central management and security of user desktops with less IT management required. You don't need desk-side support because all the apps are running remotely in the cloud. Azure Virtual Desktop provides a separate compute environment for users outside of their local device, so the chance of confidential information being left on the user device is greatly reduced. It also lets you provide standard images to users with all the tools they need already configured without having to procure hardware, set it up, and ship individual computers to users. They just access the virtual computers from their existing devices. You can choose images for Windows 11, 10, and Windows 7 with extended support until 2023, and also Server operating systems like Windows Server 2022, 2019, 2016, and 2012 R2. You can also create or upload your own image with all the software and configuration needed for users. At sign in, the user profile is dynamically attached to the computing environment and appears just like a native user profile on a local machine. Users have access to their own data, and users with privileges can even add and remove programs without impacting other users on the same remote desktops. Azure Virtual Desktop is similar to Remote Desktop Services and Windows Server, but if you've ever set up that environment in an enterprise, you know there are multiple roles and multiple servers required for scalability. You can avoid all that configuration by using Azure Virtual Desktop. So, it's really a Platform as a Service offering to provide remote virtual machines. In the past, if you wanted to provide client operating system VMs to users in Remote Desktop Services, you had to have a single VM for each user. To have multiple users use the same VM and conserve resources, you needed to use a server operating system, but Azure Virtual Desktop supports Windows 10 or 11 multi-session, which means you don't have to overprovision VMs. You can let users share the resources of a single VM. Users on a multi-session environment still have a unique secure experience, and they can use all their apps, like Office 365. The user's data and files are persisted on a separate disk that gets attached when the user logs in, so they get their desktop settings and application settings as if it's their own computer. But the user profile is separated from the operating system, so you can update the operating system and not lose the user's profile. Azure Virtual Desktop works with a couple of features that you've already learned about. You can domain join Azure Virtual Desktop VMs to Azure Active Directory Domain Services or to an existing domain in Active Directory if you've created a hybrid cloud. Azure AD provides a secure, consistent sign-on experience that allows users to roam from device to device. And it also lets you use Azure multi-factor authentication for another layer of security. Now let's move on from virtual machines and talk about hosting containers in Azure

Chapter 22 Azure Container Options

Containers are a way to wrap up an application into its own isolated package. It's for server-based applications and services, so web apps are a typical example. When an app is deployed using a container, everything the application needs to run successfully is included in the container, like runtimes and library dependencies. This makes it easy to move the container around from your local workstation to VMs in your on-premises environment that have the container runtime installed or to a managed container hosting service in Azure, like Azure Container Instances or the Azure Kubernetes Service. The main characteristic of a container is that it makes the environment the same across different deployments, so containers reduce problems with deploying applications. Let's talk about how containers are different from virtual machines. Virtual machines run on some sort of infrastructure, whether it's your laptop or it's a physical server in a datacenter in Azure. There's a host operating system that might be Windows, Linux or macOS. Then we have a hypervisor layer, and this is what runs the virtual machine and provides resources to it from the host operating system. Hyper-V is Microsoft's hypervisor technology, but there are others like VMware and KVM. Then there's the virtual machine. The virtual machine contains a full copy of an operating system, and it virtualizes the underlying hardware, meaning the CPU, memory, and storage. It also contains the application that you want to run. If you want true isolation of your applications, you'll have a copy of a VM for each application that you deploy, and that VM will need to have all the runtimes and libraries installed that the application needs. If you want to run three applications in isolation, then you'd be running three virtual machines on this hardware, each with a guest operating system that might be 800 MB in size, and each VM would require a certain amount of CPU and memory allocated to it because, again, virtual machines virtualize the hardware. Containers, on the other hand, virtualize the operating system. The host could be a physical or a virtual server, and on top of the operating system there's a runtime. This is kind of like the hypervisor for virtual machines, but it's for containers. On top of the runtime are the containers, which just contain the application along with any dependencies for that application, like frameworks and libraries for connecting storage, for example. These are the same types of things you would normally install on a VM to run your application. The containers emulate the underlying operating system rather than emulating the underlying hardware. This makes containers smaller in size than a virtual machine and quicker to spin up because you're only waiting for the app to launch, not the operating system. Because containers are so lightweight, you can host more containers on the host VM or physical server than using traditional virtual machines for each application, so there's obvious cost savings associated with that. A container is an instance of a container image. An image is a read-only template with instructions on how to create the container, and the container is the runnable instance of the image. You can create your own container images by leveraging existing images and adding the frameworks, any dependencies, and finally the code for your application. Then you can deploy the container in a repeatable way across environments. Container images get stored in a container registry. A container registry is a service that stores and distributes container images. Docker Hub is a public container registry on the web that serves as a general catalog of images. Azure offers a similar service called Azure Container Registry, which provides users with direct control of their images, integrated authentication with Azure AD, and many other features that come along with its Azure integration. I just mentioned Docker Hub. A Docker container is a standard that describes the format of containers and provides a runtime for Docker containers. Docker is an open source project that automates the deployment of containers that can run in the cloud or on-premises. Docker is also a company that promotes and evolves the technology, and they work in collaboration with cloud vendors like Microsoft. Docker has a runtime process that you can install on any workstation or VM, and there are services in Azure that provide that runtime for you. Remember that containers are portable, so they can be moved around to different hosts. Now let's talk about the different ways you can host containers. You can set up a local environment by installing the Docker runtime. Then you can develop your app locally and package up all its dependencies into the container image that you want to deploy. You could also host a container on-premises on your own hardware or virtual servers by installing the Docker runtime there. You can deploy containers on your own VMs in Azure. If you just need a small dev environment or you're not ready yet to move into container-specific services, you can still package your application into containers and deploy those onto VMs that you control. Of course, you'll need to maintain and patch those VMs, but it can at least get you started with some of the benefits that containers offer in terms of deployment and agility. With each of these approaches, you need to install the container runtime, but Azure has several Platform as a Service offerings for hosting containers. Azure Container Instances, or ACI, is a service that provides a way to host containers without having to maintain or patch the environment. It hosts a single container instance per image, so it's intended for smaller applications like simple web apps or DevTest scenarios, but it still has obvious advantages to deploying containers to your own virtual machines because you get a managed environment where you only pay for the containers. Azure Kubernetes is a fully managed container management system that can scale your application to meet demands by adding and removing container instances, as well as monitoring the deployed containers and fixing any issues that might occur. Kubernetes is an open source project, and it's one tool in a class of tools called container orchestrators. Azure Red Hat OpenShift is a service in Azure that's a partnership between Red Hat and Microsoft, and it allows for running Kubernetes powered OpenShift. If your organization is already using OpenShift, this is a way to move to a managed hosting environment in the cloud. Azure Spring Apps is for hosting containers that run Java Spring apps, so it's tailored to that specific platform. You can actually deploy containers to Azure App Service also. So in addition to deploying code onto Azure App Service, you can package web apps as containers and host them in App Service. You can also deploy containers to Azure Functions for event-driven applications. And a relatively new service in Azure for hosting containers is Azure Container Apps. This is a managed serverless container platform for running microservices. This service is also powered by Kubernetes, but it doesn't provide direct access to the underlying Kubernetes configuration, which makes management a lot easier. So the choice of how to host your containers comes down to the development platform your team uses, what orchestration platform they might be accustomed to, and how much control you want over the management of the service. Let's take a look at the simplest of the container hosting options. Azure container instances

Chapter 23 How to Create an Azure Container Instance

From All services, I'll search for container instances. There are a few other services here, like Container Registry for storing your custom containers, and Container Apps, which is another service for hosting the running of your containers. But we'll choose Azure Container Instances, a simple service for running single containers. And let's create one from the menu.

As always, we need to choose a resource group to store the metadata about the container. I'll choose the one we created earlier. Let's give this container a name, and this name only needs to be unique within the resource group. There's a lot of regions we can choose from to deploy this container instance, but I'll just leave the default. Next we can choose to deploy our container from a container registry. Azure has its own container registry service, or you could choose another service like Docker Hub, and that can be a public or a private registry with a login. But let's choose a quickstart image just to get up and running. I'll select the helloworld Linux image. And you can change the resource requirements for the container if you'd like, so the number of virtual CPUs and RAM that the container uses. Let's close this and move to the Networking tab.

Here you can create a public IP address and DNS name. So this will get prepended on the Azure service URL. You can configure environment variables here and the restart policy for the container.

Create container instance

Basics Networking Advanced Tags Review + create

Configure additional container properties and variables.

Restart policy ⓘ — On failure

Environment variables

Mark as secure — Key — Value

No

Command override ⓘ — [ ]

Example: ["/bin/bash", "-c", "echo hello; sleep 100000"]

Key management ⓘ — ⦿ Microsoft-managed keys (MMK)
○ Customer-managed keys (CMK)

This is where an orchestration service like Azure Kubernetes offers a lot more functionality. We won't add any tags. And let's create this container instance. It'll take almost a minute to create this in Azure.

And once it's created, we can navigate into the container instance. We have some monitoring happening on the Overview page.

On the Containers page, there's the container we created. It says the state is Running. Let's go back to the Overview page, and the fully qualified domain name is here on the right. This is the DNS name we added with the rest of the URL provided by Azure. Let's paste this into another browser tab.

Welcome to Azure Container Instances!

We get a basic web page that was served by the container, so we know the container is running in Azure Container Instances. Let's go back into the container on the Containers tab. And there are logs available here, so you have some visibility into the output from the container, and you can even remote into the container and get a command prompt so you can run shell commands here.

I can list out all the files and folders that are on this quickstart container.

```
/usr/src/app # ls
index.html    index.js    node_modules    package-lock.json  package.json
/usr/src/app #
```

So it's serving the default page using Node.js. That's a quick look at containers and one of the Azure services that can host them for you. Next, let's talk about Azure app service

Chapter 24 Azure App Service Fundamentals

I mentioned that you can use App Service to host containers, but it's also the Platform as a Service offering for hosting code directly, meaning the App Service is more like traditional web hosting where the frameworks are already installed on the servers, like .NET, PHP or Java, and you can deploy your code onto those servers. The difference with traditional web hosting is that Azure handles the management and patching of the underlying servers for you, but you do have lots of configuration options. Azure App Service can host web applications, API apps, which are web services that use the REST protocol, and it can host the back-end code for mobile applications, which are really just web services. You can deploy containers to Azure App Service too, but you don't have to. And there's also a feature of App Service called WebJobs that let you run services on the underlying VMs of the App Service. WebJobs can run continuously or on a schedule. They can run as executable files or they can run scripts like PowerShell or Bash scripts. So if you're running Windows services on your on-premises web servers now and wonder how you can do that in Azure, WebJobs offer that kind of functionality. There are other services in Azure to accomplish those types of tasks, and we'll look at some of them in the serverless computing section. App Service started out as a service called Azure Websites, and when you create a new App Service, the default URL is still suffixed with azurewebsites.net. And yes, you can use your own custom domain name with Azure App Service. This is just the default URL that first gets created. So an App Service is basically an individual website or API web service or mobile back end that you host. They're all really the same thing, just code that's hosted on a web server.

Before you can create an App Service, though, you need an App Service plan. The App Service plan defines the size of the underlying infrastructure, which are actually just virtual machines in Azure. But remember, you don't patch or maintain those VMs and you have limited access to them. You can run more than one App Service on a single App Service plan. When you create an App Service plan, you choose the size of the VMs, meaning the CPU, RAM, and storage by selecting the plan type, also known as the pricing tier. Depending on the pricing tier, you also have access to different features of an App Service plan. Let's create an App Service plan next and explore the features of Azure App Service in the process.

Chapter 25 How to Create an Azure App Service

We won't create an App Service plan first. We'll just do it during the creation of the App Service. I'll do that by using the shortcut on the left menu for all App Services in this subscription. Let's create a new one. And the first thing is the resource group to put this App Service in.

Let's create a new resource group for this. I'll just give it a name. And now let's give this App Service a name. This name needs to be unique across all of Azure because it's suffixed with azurewebsites.net. So this part here can't be the same as any other website on all of Azure. But remember, you can add your own domain name later. This is just the default one for creating the App Service. Next, we can choose whether to publish code or a Docker container or a static web app. For code, you choose a runtime stack, and this will be available on all the underlying web servers that the code is deployed to. The runtime you choose here will dictate which operating systems are available below. You can deploy your own Docker container from a container registry. And the Static Web App option is when you're just deploying front-end code. There's no code running on the server, so there's no runtime framework option.

This actually brings you to another service in Azure for hosting these types of static web apps, and that service uses Azure Functions for back-end logic. Static web apps integrate directly with GitHub or Azure Pipelines to pull your code, so it's a serverless environment where you don't need an underlying App Service plan. You can create one of these apps from the All services menu. It's just here is an easier way to get to that service, but it does seem a bit confusing. Let's choose a traditional code deployment, and I'll choose .NET 6, which is available on Windows and Linux VMs. Then we need to select a region where this will get deployed. If my subscription had an existing App Service plan in this region, I could choose to deploy the App Service onto that plan. But since it doesn't, a new App Service plan will get created. Because I'm using the free trial, I don't have the option to change from the free pricing tier. They're all using the free pricing tier right now because I've scaled them down to that plan to save money. Let's create a new App Service plan, and I'll give it a name.

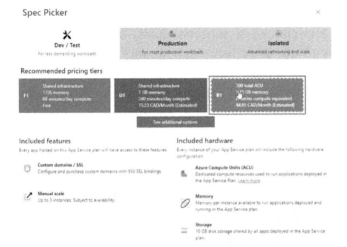

And now we can change the size, which is really changing the pricing tier. It defaults to the S1 pricing tier under the Production grouping of tiers, but we can switch to the Dev group. Below the pricing tiers are the options that are available for each one. As I change pricing tiers, features are added. With the D1 pricing tier, we can use custom domains. At B1, we can add VM instances manually when we want to scale out the resources to handle increased load. And at the S1 tier, we get autoscale and staging slots and all the features we need.

Going up from there just increases the amount of CPU, RAM, and storage on the underlying servers. So let's choose this S1 tier, and let's move to the Deployment tab. Here we can set up continuous deployment so our code gets pulled from a GitHub repository automatically.

Let's move on to Networking. We could make it so this App Service is able to call into resources in a virtual network.

Let's leave the default, though. And on the Monitoring tab, we could create an instance of Application Insights, which would collect all sorts of metrics from the App Service, like user behavior and performance of the app. But let's turn this off for now.

We can enable it after the App Service gets created. We won't create any tags, so let's create this App Service. Once it's ready, let's actually go to the tab with all the App Service plans. This is the plan that was created with the App Service. In the App Service plan, there's a tab for apps. There's only one App Service here, the one we just created. Further down the menu, you can change the pricing tier if there's features you need to use or you just need more powerful VMs.

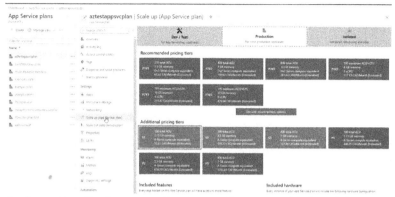

And on the Scale out tab, depending on which pricing tier you're on, you can add VMs to the plan. And, of course, there are costs associated with that.

And you can also configure autoscaling. So when a certain metric is reached, more VMs will be added. In the list here, there are lots of metrics you can have the App Service plan watch, like the amount of CPU being used, the disk queue length, and the percentage of RAM being used. Then you can configure some logic to add or remove VMs under certain conditions.

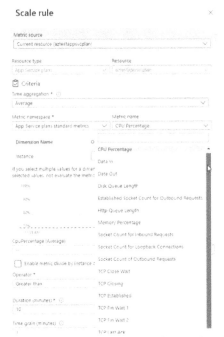

Let's close this, and let's go back to the Apps tab and drill into the App Service we created. So this is a web app that can use .NET for its server-side logic. We haven't deployed any code here, but there is a default page created for you that you can access from this Browse button. That opens up a tab with the URL that we chose during creation, so we know that the servers are running and serving content.

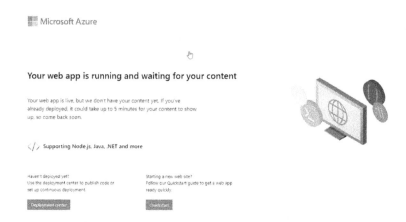

Back in the App Service, let's explore some of the things we can configure. You can add a custom domain.

You can either purchase that through a third party and just verify it here in which case you'd need to point your DNS provider to this IP address or to the URL that you saw on the browse page depending on the type of DNS record that you use, or you can actually buy an App Service domain through

Azure right here in the portal. Let's look at the Configuration tab. This lets you add name value pairs that can be read by your application code. You can also add connection strings to databases here. This lets you keep configuration and secrets out of your code.

If you've written ASP.NET applications before, you know there's a configuration file in your project. Any values here with the same name as what's in that file will override the values in the file, so administrators can manage configuration in the portal. Notice there's a checkbox for deployment slot settings. Deployment slots let you create different environments like dev, user acceptance testing, and production.

So you can have a different version of your web app in each of them, and you can promote your web app through the environments from right here in the portal, and the application settings and database connection strings that we saw can be unique to each deployment slot. So the code gets promoted and the values change for each environment. Now let's take a look at authentication. One of the great things about Azure App Service is that you can let it handle authentication for you. You just choose the provider that your user base uses, and you can use multiple providers.

Add an identity provider

Basics   Permissions

Choose an identity provider from the dropdown below to start.

Identity provider *   Select identity provider

Microsoft
Sign in Microsoft and Azure AD identities and call Microsoft APIs

Apple
Sign in Apple users and call Apple APIs

Facebook
Sign in Facebook users and call Facebook APIs

GitHub
Sign in GitHub users and call GitHub APIs

Google
Sign in Google users and call Google APIs

Twitter
Sign in Twitter users and call Twitter APIs

OpenID Connect
Sign in users with OpenID Connect

You could use Azure Active Directory, so accounts need to exist there. Or you could use outside authentication providers, like Facebook, Twitter, or pretty much any service that uses this protocol called OpenID Connect. That works with OAuth 2.0, which is a standard on the web. Remember we talked about that when we talked about Azure Active Directory Domain Services. One of the scary things about turning over management of your web servers to a third party, even Microsoft, is how do you troubleshoot that when there's a problem? Same with a deployment. You don't have access to the file system directly, but you can turn on quite a bit of logging, including logs from the web server and from the application.

Those can get stored in Azure Storage as files, or you can have them written onto the local server in the App Service plan, in which case you can actually stream them from here and see the logging in real time. You can stream the logs onto your local computer using Visual Studio or PowerShell also. There's a lot more here that can help you with troubleshooting. Under the advanced tools, there's a link to the Kudu portal. That's an application that gets installed with your App Service that provides all sorts of information about the environment like system information and environment variables on the servers.

Under the Tools menu, there's a way you can deploy your web app by dragging a zip file containing the website right into the browser here. There are a lot of other ways to deploy apps to Azure App Service too, but we'll stop here. Next, we'll look at serverless computing in Azure and Azure Functions in particular.

Chapter 26 Serverless Computing in Azure

There's always servers involved in Azure. The term just really refers to how little you might need to interact with those servers. Serverless computing is about letting developers focus on the code and business logic that they're developing and not on the underlying infrastructure. The environment is set up for you, and it scales automatically to meet demand, but you don't need to do any configuration to make that happen, even the minimal config you need to do with App Service or virtual machine scale sets. Serverless computing also differs from the other compute models you've seen in that you're only charged when the code runs, so you don't need a virtual machine or an App Service running, waiting to do the work. The two main services in Azure that are considered serverless computing are Azure Functions and Azure Logic Apps. Logic Apps don't really fall under the Azure compute category. They are now categorized as part of the integration category of services, but they're used so often with Azure Functions that it's worth mentioning here. Both of these services can be used independently, but are often used together to build solutions. Azure Functions allow you to run small pieces of code that you write yourself. Functions are started by triggers, which could be an HTTP call to the function endpoint, an event that happens in another Azure service, like a blob getting created in Azure Storage, or you can run the code based on a timer event. You can write functions in C#, Java, JavaScript, TypeScript, Python, and even in PowerShell. Azure Functions can run completely serverless, and this is called the consumption-based model. But if you already have an Azure App Service plan that you're paying for, you can also leverage that to host Azure Functions. Azure Logic Apps allow you to design workflows right in the Azure portal, so you don't need to write any code with Logic Apps. You can automate business processes when you need to integrate apps, data, and services. Logic Apps have a huge library of connectors to everything from SharePoint and Azure Storage to Zendesk and SAP. When there isn't a built-in connector that suits your requirements, you can always write code in an Azure Function and call it from a Logic App. So even though Logic Apps are very powerful, it's always good to know that when you hit a wall in terms of functionality, there's a way to write code to accomplish what you need. So for an example of how these can work together, you could create a Logic App that watches an email account for an email with attachments, then cleanses the body of the email using an Azure Function. Then the Logic App could create a blob in an Azure storage account and store the email and the attachment there. In terms of choosing one over the other, if you need a solution that calls well-known APIs, Logic Apps are a good place to start because of all the connectors available. If your solution needs to execute custom algorithms or do special data lookups, Azure Functions would be a starting place because you already know that you need to write code. Let's create an Azure Function next.

Chapter 27 How to Create an Azure Function

This will just be a simple HTTP trigger that returns HTML to the browser. I'll start by going to All services and searching for Function Apps.

A Function App is the container that holds multiple functions. Click Create, and we get brought to the creation screen. Let's create this Function App in the resource group.

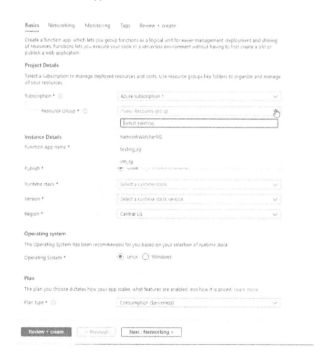

We need to give this Function App a name. And similar to Azure App Services, this name needs to be unique across Azure because it's suffixed with azurewebsites.net. So you can start to see the relationship here between Function Apps and Web Apps in the Azure App Service. Next, we select to deploy code or a container. Because I'm using the free trial subscription here, only code is available. I'll select the runtime stack as .NET, but you can see there are other options here, like Node.js and Java. I'll leave the default framework version, .NET 6, and I'll leave the default region too. You can deploy Function Apps onto Linux or Windows. It just depends on the runtime stack you've selected. .NET runs on both, but not all the frameworks do. And the plan is the most important thing here.

The consumption-based plan will take care of all the sizing and scaling of the VMs for us, and we'll only be charged based on when the functions are called. The other options are grayed out because I'm using the free Azure trial. But normally, you can select to create this Function App on an existing App Service plan right alongside your other web apps and API apps. Or you can choose the Function Premium plan, which adds some network and connectivity options and avoids having to warm up the underlying VMs, so the performance can be better.

Create Function App

Basics **Networking** Monitoring Tags Review + create

Function Apps can be provisioned with the inbound address being public to the internet or isolated to an Azure virtual network. Function Apps can also be provisioned with outbound traffic able to reach endpoints in a virtual network, be governed by network security groups or affected by virtual network routes. By default, your app is open to the internet and cannot reach into a virtual network. These aspects can also be changed after the app is provisioned. Learn more

⚠ Network injection is only available in Functions Premium And Basic, Standard, Premium, Premium V2, Premium V3 Dedicated App Service plans.

Enable network injection   ◯ On ◉ Off

And this is where the Function Premium plan provides networking options to restrict access to only virtual networks, not the public internet. On the Monitoring tab, we have the option to enable Application Insights for deep monitoring, just like with App Services.

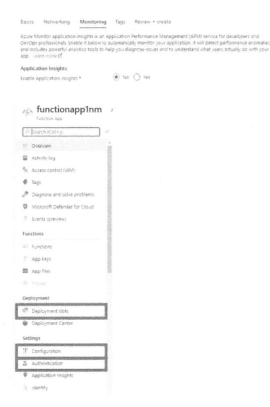

Create Function App

Basics Networking **Monitoring** Tags Review + create

Azure Monitor application insights is an Application Performance Management (APM) service for developers and DevOps professionals. Enable it below to automatically monitor your application. It will detect performance anomalies and includes powerful analytics tools to help you diagnose issues and to understand what users actually do with your app. Learn more

Application Insights

Enable Application Insights *   ◉ No ◯ Yes

functionapp1nm
Function App

🔍 Search (Ctrl+/)

⊙ Overview
📋 Activity log
🔒 Access control (IAM)
🏷 Tags
🩺 Diagnose and solve problems
🛡 Microsoft Defender for Cloud
⚡ Events (preview)

Functions

⌨ Functions
🔑 App keys
📄 App files
⊕ Proxies

Deployment

🗂 Deployment slots
🚀 Deployment Center

Settings

⚙ Configuration
🔐 Authentication
📊 Application Insights
🆔 Identity

Once it's created, let's navigate into the Function App. So this looks a lot like an App Service already. There are deployment slots, configuration, authentication, and custom domains. But under the Function grouping, there's this Functions tab, and there aren't any functions yet. So again, the Function App is the container, and you can have multiple functions here. Okay, now let's create the function.

The first thing is the development environment. You can develop functions using VS Code or another editor with core tools installed like Visual Studio. Or you can develop right here in the portal in the editor. So let's just stick with that. Next, we choose the type of trigger, so what's going to cause this function to run? It could be an HTTP call to the endpoint, it could run on a timer, or this Function App could watch for events in Azure, like when a blob is added to a specific container in Azure Storage or a document changes in a Cosmos DB database. Let's go with the HTTP trigger.

This is how you would call the function from another program, like a Logic App for example. We can change the function's name, and we can choose the authorization level. This has to do with whether or not the caller needs to supply a key, which is just a shared secret.

So you can prevent unauthorized callers from causing this function to run and costing you money. Let's just leave it wide open for the example though, and let's create this function. Once it's created, we're brought into the function. We've got some options along the left here.

Let's click Code + Test. That opens up the editor where you can modify the default code. This just gives you a starting place to see how the function is structured. The default code will write to the log, and it will look for a string in the query string value and send back a response over HTTP. You can write some really complex functions to interact with other services and perform whatever logic you want to code. But this is an easy-to-understand example, so let's just stick with this. Next on the menu is the Integration tab where you can see how the function is laid out and make modifications here. This is just an overview, so we won't go into this. But let's go back to the code and test, and let's run this function.

Let's copy the function URL. So this is the endpoint that the caller would use. They could do that programmatically to get the results back, but let's open up a new browser tab and paste this in. I'll increase the font size.

This HTTP triggered function executed successfully. Pass a name in the query string or in the request body for a personalized response.

It says the function ran successfully and that we can pass a name in the query string. So functions are an easy way to deploy small packages of business logic onto a managed environment and can provide cost savings over hosting a full-blown app service. In summary, you learned about computer options in Azure, starting with the service delivery models, then looking at virtual machines, containers, Azure App Service, and Azure Functions. Next, we'll look at networking in Azure.

Chapter 28 Azure Networking

Azure has a number of products for networking that allow you to create secure networks for your virtual machines and other Azure resources so those resources can communicate with each other and with the internet. The underlying physical network and components are managed by Microsoft, and you configure virtual versions of everything that you need. An Azure virtual network is a fundamental building block for your private network. A VNet enables many types of Azure resources to communicate. A virtual network has an address space that you define in Azure, which is a group of IP addresses that can be assigned to resources like virtual machines. A VNet is segmented into one or more subnetworks called subnets, which are allocated a portion of the VNet's IP address space. Then you deploy Azure resources to a specific subnet. A VM is assigned to a subnet, and VMs can communicate with other VMs on the same network. But you can apply security rules to that traffic using network security groups, or NSGs. These allow you to filter network traffic by allowing or denying traffic into and out of the subnet. Virtual machines are deployed into virtual networks, but you can also deploy other Azure resources into a VNet, networking components, like Azure Firewall, Application Gateway, and VPN Gateway. You can deploy data-related resources like Redis Cache and Azure SQL Managed Instances, and analytics resources, like Azure HDInsight and Azure Databricks. And Azure Kubernetes Service gets deployed into a VNet also. You can also configure App Services to have a private IP on your VNet, which enables private connections to App Services, which have traditionally only been available over the internet. By default, resources assigned to one virtual network can't communicate with resources in another virtual network. So there's some inherent security controls built in, but you can enable that communication between virtual networks using a feature called VNet peering. You can enable VNet peering between virtual networks in the same region, as well as VNets in different Azure regions, and the traffic flows privately over Microsoft's backbone network. You can connect an on-premises network to an Azure virtual network also using a VPN gateway or using a service called ExpressRoute. Virtual machines on a VNet can communicate out to the internet by default. But in order for inbound communications to take place from the internet, the virtual machine needs to be assigned to public IP address. Technically, the public IP address gets attached to the network interface of the virtual machine. So each of these is a separate resource in Azure with their own configuration. I mentioned network security groups, or NSGs. You also use these to control the inbound and outbound traffic to the internet. You can assign a network security group to the subnet or directly to the network interface of a VM. Then you can filter traffic with rules based on the source and destination IP addresses, the ports being accessed, and the protocol being used, like TCP or UDP. Now let's talk about load balancing in Azure. In order to distribute traffic between virtual machines for high availability, you can create a load balancer. There are public load balancers in Azure, which load balance internet traffic to your VMs. You can actually use a public load balancer to allow traffic to your VM without needing to attach a public IP address to the VM. And there are also internal or private load balancers where traffic is coming from inside the network. A public load balancer can provide inbound connections to VMs for traffic coming from the internet. It can translate the public IP address to the private IP addresses of the VMs inside a VNet.

It's a high-performance solution that can handle a lot of traffic, but it's just a load balancing and port forwarding engine. It doesn't interact with the traffic coming in. It just checks the health of the back-end resources. When you're exposing resources to the internet, particularly servers on your internal virtual network, you usually want more control over the traffic. That's where Azure Application Gateway can offer more features and security for publishing applications to the internet. Application Gateway is a web traffic load balancer that exposes a public IP to the internet, and it can do things like SSL termination. So traffic between the client and the App Gateway is encrypted, but then the traffic between App Gateway and the back-end virtual machines can flow unencrypted, which unburdens the VMs from costly encryption and decryption overhead. App Gateway supports autoscaling, so it can scale up and down depending on traffic load patterns. It supports session affinity for applications that require a user to return to the same web server after they've started a session. It can do rewriting of HTTP headers and can make routing decisions based on more than just the IP address and the port that was requested. And App Gateway also uses a service called Web Application Firewall, which protects your web applications from common exploits and vulnerabilities like SQL injection attacks and cross-site scripting. So again, Application Gateway is more than just a load balancer. If you search for load balancing in the Azure portal, you'll see descriptions of all the options. Besides Load Balancer and Application Gateway, there are two other options that relate to load balancing across different regions.

Traffic Manager allows you to distribute traffic to services across global Azure regions. Front Door has more capabilities for application delivery. We'll look a little closer at some of the major components of virtual networking in Azure. We'll create a virtual network and subnets. Then we'll create a virtual machine and attach it to the existing VNet. Next, you'll see how to use network security groups to allow traffic to the VM from the internet. After that, we'll peer two virtual networks so the VMs on the VNets can communicate. Then we'll discuss the options for connecting on-premises networks to Azure using VPN Gateway and then ExpressRoute. Next, we'll discuss Azure DNS for managing DNS services alongside your other Azure resources. And finally, we'll talk about private endpoints in Azure, which bring platform services like App Services and storage accounts into your private virtual network. So next, let's create a virtual network.

Chapter 29 How to Create an Azure VNET

I'll start by going to All services and searching for virtual network.

Click this, and there aren't any created yet, so I'll click Create. As always, we need a resource group. I'm going to create a new one, so I'll just give it a name, and let's call this vnet1, and I'll place it in the closest region to me. Next, let's configure the IP address space for this VNet.

This is called CIDR notation. The number after the slash tells how many addresses are in the range, starting at the number before the slash. So a /16 means there are about 64,000 IPs available in the address space. We can assign these IP addresses to virtual machines and other services that can be addressed within a VNet. When you configure your IP address space, the IP addresses are private to your VNet. The only time it matters is when you want to connect this VNet with another network, like another VNet in Azure using peering or with your local network on-premises using VPN Gateway or ExpressRoute. In that case, those IP addresses can't overlap with this address space. We can break this up into smaller blocks of IP addresses using subnets, and then we can apply security to a subnet. I'll call this WebSubnet because I want to put web servers in this subnet. I'll give it an address range that starts within the range of the VNet and has a smaller block of IP addresses. In CIDR notation, a larger number means a smaller group of IPs. So a /27 is only 32 IP addresses. We can attach service endpoints to the subnet.

Service endpoints allow traffic to specific services in Azure over the Microsoft backbone. So VMs on the subnet could connect to Azure SQL or Azure Storage without having to connect to the public endpoints on the internet. Let's create this subnet, and let's create another subnet. Let's call this AppSubnet. So I might put application servers on this subnet and have them only accessible from VMs on the web subnet. Then you can use network security groups to enforce that. I'll give this subnet a range that starts higher than the highest IP available in the WebSubnet. And let's make this a /24, so there are 256 IP addresses available on this subnet.

Create virtual network

Let's add this, and let's move on to the Security tab. Here, you can enable a bastion host, which is a VM that lets you remote into the virtual machines in this VNet without having to connect to them directly, so that's for security. We can enable DDOS standard protection.

Create virtual network

Every VNet comes with basic protection against distributed denial of service attacks. By enabling standard protection, you get additional metrics and access to experts within

Microsoft if an attack is launched against one of your applications. That comes for an additional charge, which is why you have to enable this. Azure Firewall is an intelligent firewall security service. It can watch for patterns and alert you to traffic coming from known malicious IP addresses and domains and deny that traffic. But let's leave these off, and let's move ahead and create this VNet.

Once the VNet is created, I'll go to the shortcut to all VNets. On the menu here, you can see the IP address space we configured, and you can modify it from here.

You can create and remove subnets. And down here, you can specify the DNS servers to use. You can let Azure handle DNS resolution for you, or you can add the IP address of your own DNS servers.

DNS resolves domain names to the IP addresses of servers, so you might create your own network in a VNet with a VM for Active Directory, VMs for applications, and a VM for hosting DNS services. You might do that if you're setting up a lab environment in Azure here, for example. Setting that VM as the DNS server here will allow all the VMs on the network to resolve your internal domain names to the IPs of the servers, but you can actually use a service called Azure DNS for that also. And on the tab for peerings, you can peer this VNet with other VNets in Azure, so the VMs and resources can communicate. If you have any resources that have been assigned IP addresses on the VNet, their network interfaces will show up here. We don't have any, so let's create a virtual machine next and add it to this VNet.

Chapter 30 How to Add Virtual Machine to VNET

So we have a VNet, but it doesn't have anything on it. So let's create a virtual machine just like we did earlier, but this time, we won't create a new virtual network at the same time. We'll add the VM to the existing VNet. We went through all this earlier, so I'll move quickly through this. Let's put this VM in the same resource group as the VNet. We don't have to, but that'll make it easier to delete everything at once later. But this VM does need to be in the same region as the VNet. Let's turn off the availability options and change the VM image from Linux to Windows Server.

I need to enter a username and password for the local administrator account. Now let's move to the Disks tab, and I'll leave the defaults.

Create a virtual machine

And Networking is where I want to assign this VM to the existing VNet. Remember the VM is being created in the same Azure region as the VNet is in so that VNet is available in the drop-down list here.

You also need to select which subnet to put this virtual machine on. Technically, it's the network interface attached to this VM that will get the IP address from the subnet. The default for security is that a network security group will get created and assigned to the network interface of this VM. But we're going to create a separate network security group and assign it to the subnet, not to the VM. So I'll turn this off for now. That's all I want to change in the defaults, so let's skip ahead through these tabs and create this VM. It'll take a minute or so to create this, and once the VM is created, let's navigate into it from here. I'll go to the Connect screen.

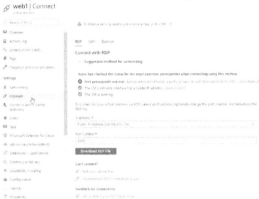

This is where we downloaded the RDP file to connect into the VM. It says here that the port prerequisite is not met. That's because there's no network security group that will allow traffic to this VM from the internet. Let's download the RDP file and try to connect anyway just to be sure. I'll open the file and click Connect, and I don't even get to the login screen because Azure won't allow the connection to the VM over port 3389.

So let's fix that in the next chapter.

Chapter 31 How to Create a Network Security Group (NSG)

We can't connect into this VM from outside the Azure VNet. Let's fix that by creating a network security group, or NSG, and opening up port 3389 to the internet. I'll go to All services again and search for network security. Click on Network security groups, and there aren't any yet in the subscription. This is a different subscription from the free trial that I used earlier in the course when I created that VM. Otherwise, the network security group attached to the network interface of that VM would show up here. I'll create a new network security group. We need to put this in a resource group, so I'll use the same one as the VNet and the VM, and that updates the region for me. And I'll give this a descriptive name.

That's all the configuration you can do when you create the NSG, so let's skip tags and create this. Once the NSG is created, let's navigate into the resource. On the Overview tab, it shows the default inbound and outbound security rules.

Network security groups allow you to permit or deny traffic between sources and destinations and to be specific about which ports and which protocol are permitted or denied. Before we add an inbound rule to allow port 3389 from the internet, let's just verify that this NSG isn't attached to a network interface for a virtual machine. If it was, that would show here. And this isn't associated with any subnets either, so let's do that first.

I'll select the VNet that's in the same region as this NSG, which is the one we want and then associate this with the subnet that the VM is on, which is the WebSubnet. Now the security rules of this network security group are being applied to the subnet that the VM is on. So let's go to Inbound security rules, and let's add a new rule. I won't go through each of these options. But if you wanted to allow HTTP traffic from the internet to a web server in the subnet associated with this NSG, you would allow ports 80 to the IP address of the VM or to any VM on the subnet, which is the default here, Let's do something similar, but allowing RDP traffic, which changes the port to 3389.

And that's all we need to do. So let's just change the name of the security rule and add it to the NSG. Now it shows at the top of the list because it has higher priority than the other rules.

These rules are processed based on priority, the lower number taking precedence. So this RDP rule overrides the rule at the bottom to deny all inbound traffic. Now let's go back to the list of virtual machines and drill into this VM and go to the Connect tab.

Now it shows that the inbound access port check past, so we should be able to connect using RDP. Let's download the RDP file, although we could use the one we downloaded before. Nothing's really changed. And I'm getting brought to the login screen, so that's progress. I'll enter the credentials of the local administrator on this VM. Okay, I can accept the certificate errors, and I'm brought into the remote desktop of the virtual machine in Azure. So the network security group enabled access from the internet from my local computer. Let's just wait until the connection is completed. Now I'll open up the command prompt, and let's run the ipconfig command. This shows us the IP address of this VM. It's been assigned an IP address on the subnet of vnet1.

```
Windows IP Configuration

Ethernet adapter Ethernet:

   Connection-specific DNS Suffix  . : v2tz0ozeg5ue3cjrd53al0155h.ux.internal.cloudapp.net
   Link-local IPv6 Address . . . . . : fe80::c5b1:4bca:c158:d42d%6
   IPv4 Address. . . . . . . . . . . : 10.20.0.4
   Subnet Mask . . . . . . . . . . . : 255.255.255.224
   Default Gateway . . . . . . . . . : 10.20.0.1
```

Next, let's see how to set up VNet peering, so this VM can access a VM on another VNet.

Chapter 32 How to Peer Virtual Networks

Now let's see how to allow resources in different virtual networks to communicate with each other by peering the virtual networks. I've created another VNet for this demo. The type is kind of small here, but the VNets have different address spaces, and the IP addresses in each address space don't overlap.

I've also created another virtual machine. And if I drill into it, it shows here that the VM network interface is attached to a different VNet and subnet. The private IP address of this VM on the VNet is 10.0.0.4. Let's remember that.

I've still got the Remote Desktop window open to the VM on the other network, the one that we created earlier. Let's open up the command prompt. It still shows the results of ipconfig, which shows that this VM is on the first VNet, vnet1. Let's try and ping the VM on the other VNet. I've turned off the firewall on that VM by the way, so it will allow ICMP traffic, which is what ping uses. The request is timing out as expected.

```
Pinging 10.0.0.4 with 32 bytes of data:
Request timed out.
Request timed out.
```

Let's go to all virtual networks, and let's go into vent1. You can actually do this from either direction, vnet1 or vnet2. Let's go to Peerings on the menu and add a peering.

I'll give this link a descriptive name to show what it's meant to do, and the default is to allow traffic between the VNets. It's going to create a peering in the other VNet, so we need to give that one a name too. And now let's select the VNet to peer with. I'll select vnet2 and accept the defaults, and let's add this peering. That's all there is to it.

It says the status is connected. Let's navigate to vnet2 from the link here, and let's go to Peerings, and there's the other side of the peering.

Now let's see if we can ping the virtual machine in vnet2 from the virtual machine in vnet1. I'll open up the Remote Desktop session again, and I'll just press the up arrow key to show the last command and hit Enter. Now the ping is working, so we successfully peered the two VNets.

```
Pinging 10.0.0.4 with 32 bytes of data:
Reply from 10.0.0.4: bytes=32 time=2ms TTL=128
Reply from 10.0.0.4: bytes=32 time<1ms TTL=128
Reply from 10.0.0.4: bytes=32 time<1ms TTL=128
Reply from 10.0.0.4: bytes=32 time<1ms TTL=128

Ping statistics for 10.0.0.4:
    Packets: Sent = 4, Received = 4, Lost = 0 (0% loss),
Approximate round trip times in milli-seconds:
    Minimum = 0ms, Maximum = 2ms, Average = 0ms
```

So that's how you can allow VNets in Azure to communicate with each other. Next, let's see how to allow on-premises networks to communicate with resources in Azure VNets.

Chapter 33 Azure VPN Gateway Basics

When you want to connect your on-premises network to an Azure VNet, there are a couple of ways to do it. In this chapter, we'll talk about VPN gateways, and in the next, we'll talk about Azure ExpressRoute. What does it mean to connect your networks? It means that from the computers and servers joined to your on-premises network, you can access the virtual machines and other Azure resources that have private IP addresses on that VNet in Azure. To the users on your local network, there's no difference accessing an application on a web server in Azure than there is accessing one on the local network, and that web server in Azure doesn't need to be exposed to the internet. The connection from on-premises is taking place over a private secure connection. To make that connection between networks, you can use a VPN gateway in Azure. VPN Gateway creates a private encrypted tunnel over the public internet. If you connect to your local office now using a VPN, it's basically the same thing. Azure VPN Gateway is made up of one or more VMs that get deployed into a subnet in your Azure VNet. That subnet needs to have a specific name, and you can't configure the VMs for the gateway subnet. You connect to the VPN gateway through its public IP address. If you're connecting your entire on-premises network to Azure, then the VPN gateway needs to connect to a VPN device on your network that has a public IP address to the internet. The traffic between the on-premises network and the Azure VNet flows through the gateway. There are a few different types of connections. Let's take a look at the documentation to see some diagrams.

Site-to-Site VPN

A Site-to-Site (S2S) VPN gateway connection is a connection over IPsec/IKE (IKEv1 or IKEv2) VPN tunnel. S2S connections can be used for cross-premises and hybrid configurations. A S2S connection requires a VPN device located on-premises that has a public IP address assigned to it. For information about selecting a VPN device, see the VPN Gateway FAQ - VPN devices.

You can create a VPN gateway that connects to your on-premises network. One major stipulation is that you have to make sure that the IP address ranges of the VNet in Azure don't overlap with your on-premises IP addresses. A virtual network in Azure can only have one VPN gateway, but you can make multiple connections to it.

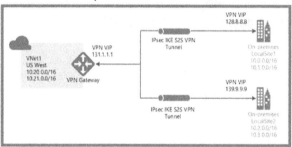

So if you have different regional offices with different networks, you can connect them to the same VPN gateway and the same VNet in Azure. There's a second type of connection possible, which is called a point-to-site VPN. This is where a single computer connects to the VPN gateway.

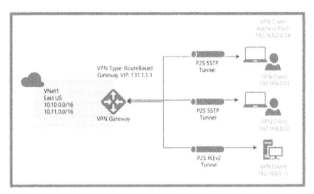

You might use this if you're working from home. It doesn't require the local computer to have a public IP address or a VPN server, like with the site-to-site VPN, but you need to authenticate using certificates uploaded to Azure and on your local computer. It's also possible to use VPN Gateway to set up a connection between two VNets in Azure.

That's an alternate to VNet peering. You might do this if you have older VNets in Azure that were created with the classic deployment model, and you want to join them with newer VNets that use the resource manager model. You can't have more than one VPN gateway in an Azure VNet, but you can connect to a VNet using both VPN Gateway and ExpressRoute. The difference is that VPN Gateway uses the public internet, and ExpressRoute uses a private connection that's not over the public internet.

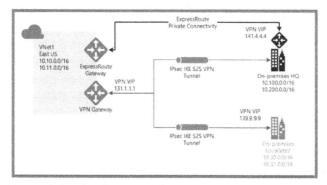

You might do this in order to use VPN Gateway as a failover if, for some reason, the ExpressRoute connection isn't available. That's a lot cheaper than maintaining a backup ExpressRoute connection.

Chapter 34 Azure ExpressRoute Basics

The other type of connection you can make from your on-premises network to Azure is an ExpressRoute connection. The connection is made through a third-party service provider that's partnered with Microsoft. You connect to the service provider, and they connect directly to the Microsoft edge servers. So the traffic doesn't get routed over the public internet. There are actually two ExpressRoute circuits created, so there's built-in redundancy. ExpressRoute can connect your network to multiple VNets in Azure, which is called private peering. You can also connect to Azure public services, like App Service endpoints and storage accounts, as well as Microsoft 365, which used to be called Office 365, and Dynamics 365, which is a Software as a Service customer relationship management system. This type of connection used to be called public peering, but it's now called Microsoft peering. ExpressRoute requires you to work with a third-party provider, and they're partnered with Microsoft to connect to Azure. These providers have infrastructure at data centers where they're collocated with Microsoft edge servers. Examples of these providers are companies like AT&T or Verizon, but there are many regional providers, and they're listed on docs.microsoft.com by location. Each ExpressRoute circuit has a fixed bandwidth, and you choose a plan between 50 Mbps and 10 Gbps. The speeds available depend on the service provider that you work with. There's also something called ExpressRoute Direct where you can establish a direct connection to Microsoft's global network at peering locations around the world. This gives you increased speed and encryption options and, of course, increased cost. So ExpressRoute direct is for big corporate clients with major security requirements like banks and government. You can choose to be charged based on how much data you transfer out of Azure, which is metered billing. Inbound data is always free, or you can pay a monthly fee for unlimited data. The standard ExpressRoute plan gives you access to all the regions in a geopolitical area, but there are two other plans available. The local plan gives you access to only one or two Azure regions near the location where you're peering. You don't pay additional charges for egress for the data coming out of Azure, so this can be economical for large data transfers. And the ExpressRoute Premium add-on gives you global connectivity to any region in the world. So if there's a lot of data moving between your on-premises network and Azure, ExpressRoute can give you the best performance. Let's talk about Azure DNS next.

Chapter 35 Azure DNS Basics

Azure DNS is a way to manage your DNS records right in Azure alongside all your other Azure resources. First, let's review what DNS is. When you create a service in Azure, like an App Service or an Azure Function, they get a name that's suffixed with azurewebsites.net. And when you create a VM, there's a public IP address. You can also add a DNS name label to the public IP address of the VM right in the Azure portal, so you don't have to use the IP address to access it. But again, it ends in an address that you don't control. It's the region name, then cloudapp.azure.com. But when you're publishing your applications for clients, you'll want a custom domain name. Usually, your application name .com or .net or ending in a region-specific suffix, like .ca for Canada. You purchase the custom domain name from a domain registrar, and they're responsible to make sure that no one else owns the domain name. If it's available, you pay an annual fee to reserve the use of the domain name. There are a lot of domain registrars, and the biggest one is GoDaddy. Once you own the domain name, it needs to be hosted by a DNS provider. DNS stands for domain name system, and it's the network of DNS servers all over the world that resolve domain names to the IP addresses of the servers that host the corresponding applications. Your DNS provider makes sure that all those servers can find your domain name and resolve it. Often, when you purchase a domain name, that same company, like GoDaddy, will often let you host the DNS entries with them, but you don't have to. You can host them with any DNS service, and that's what Azure DNS is. Azure DNS is a hosting service for DNS domains that provides name resolution by using Microsoft Azure infrastructure. That's the definition right from the Microsoft docs. Azure isn't a domain registrar. Azure doesn't register your domain name, but they can manage the DNS for it. You can actually purchase domains in Azure using a service called App Service Domains. But App Service Domains actually use GoDaddy for the domain registration and Azure DNS to host the domain name resolution. So you can purchase app service domains for Azure App Services, and everything gets configured for you to point the domain name to the app service. But because they're managed by Azure DNS, you can actually modify the DNS records to point the domain to another Azure service, like a virtual machine or an Azure storage account. If you host your domain name with another DNS provider, you can transfer it to Azure DNS. Then you can manage the DNS records alongside all your other Azure resources, which means you can enable role-based access control to control who in your organization has access, and you can get activity logs to monitor when records are modified, which can help with troubleshooting. DNS domains are hosted on Azure's global network of DNS name servers so that helps with reliability and performance. Besides managing DNS for public domains so they can be resolved from the internet, Azure DNS can also support private DNS domains. That means you can use your own custom DNS domains in your private virtual networks rather than have to set up your own DNS servers on your VM on your VNet. It's great to be able to manage public and private domains in one place. Azure DNS also supports alias record sets. That means you can use an alias record to refer to an Azure resource, like the public IP address of a VM or a content delivery endpoint. Then, if the IP address changes, Azure automatically updates the records. If you manage your DNS records outside of Azure, you might not update those records right away if there's a change in Azure, and then users won't be able to access your service. So having that be automatic with Azure DNS can be really helpful. Next, let's talk about private endpoints.

Chapter 36 Azure Private Endpoints

Private endpoints allow you to essentially bring a public Azure service into your own VNet, so the service can get referenced with a private IP address. When you create a service in Azure, like an App Service, it has public endpoints. That means there's an address on the internet where that resource can be reached. For App Service, that's a URL, the name of your App Service, then azurewebsites.net. That resolves to an IP address. But in certain situations, that IP address can actually change, like during the renewal of an SSL certificate. So really it's the URL that's the endpoint. Azure takes care of the resolution to the underlying IP address for other services, like Azure Storage. You can go to the Endpoints tab and see the public endpoints for your instance of the service. In this case, the endpoint is the name of your storage account, then the individual service in Azure Storage, like the Blob Service, File Service, or Queue Service, and then it's always core.windows.net. These endpoints allow people to reach the blobs and files in the particular service from the internet, but you'll see that you can apply security to the endpoint But, what about if you don't want your App Service or storage account to be accessible from the internet? You only want resources on your own Azure VNet to be able to access the service, so virtual machines on your VNet. Or if you've connected your on-premises network to an Azure VNet, you want your users to be able to access the App Service or storage account only through that secure connection and then disable access from the public internet. You can do that by creating a private endpoint for the Azure service. A private endpoint is a network interface that uses a private IP address on your virtual network. So the App Service or storage account gets a private IP address on your

VNet, and you can access it privately and securely using that IP address. For some services, like Azure App Service, creating a private endpoint will automatically prevent access to the public endpoint, so from the internet. For other services like Azure storage, the public internet access isn't automatically disabled, but you can configure that yourself. Private endpoints use a service called Azure Private Link. With Azure Private Link, you can create connections to Azure Platform as a Service offering, and your connection between your VNet and the service travels over the Microsoft backbone network. In order to create a private link to an Azure service, the service has to support it. On docs.microsoft.com, you can see a list of all the resources in Azure that support private link.

Private-link resource

A private-link resource is the destination target of a specified private endpoint. The following table lists the available resources that support a private endpoint:

Private-link resource name	Resource type	Subresources
Azure App Configuration	Microsoft.AppConfiguration/configurationStores	configurationStores
Azure Automation	Microsoft.Automation/automationAccounts	Webhook, DSCAndHybridWorker
Azure Cosmos DB	Microsoft.AzureCosmosDB/databaseAccounts	SQL, MongoDB, Cassandra, Gremlin, Table
Azure Batch	Microsoft.Batch/batchAccounts	batchAccount, nodeManagement
Azure Cache for Redis	Microsoft.Cache/Redis	redisCache
Azure Cache for Redis Enterprise	Microsoft.Cache/redisEnterprise	redisEnterprise
Azure Cognitive Services	Microsoft.CognitiveServices/accounts	account
Azure Managed Disks	Microsoft.Compute/diskAccesses	managed disk
Azure Container Registry	Microsoft.ContainerRegistry/registries	registry
Azure Kubernetes Service - Kubernetes API	Microsoft.ContainerService/managedClusters	management
Azure Data Factory	Microsoft.DataFactory/factories	dataFactory
Azure Data Explorer	Microsoft.Kusto/clusters	cluster
Azure Database for MariaDB	Microsoft.DBforMariaDB/servers	mariadbServer
Azure Database for MySQL	Microsoft.DBforMySQL/servers	mysqlServer
Azure Database for PostgreSQL - Single server	Microsoft.DBforPostgreSQL/servers	postgresqlServer
Azure Device Provisioning Service	Microsoft.Devices/provisioningServices	iotDps

So besides App Services and storage accounts, Azure Cosmos DB supports private endpoints, Azure Container Registry, Azure Service Bus, Azure SQL Database. So chances are if you want to create a private endpoint to a platform as a service offering in Azure, it's probably possible to do it. Let's quickly see how to set up a private endpoint for an App Service. I'll open up the App Service we created earlier. If you go to the Networking menu item, you can configure some options here, including private endpoints.

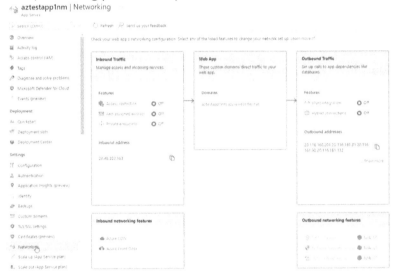

This is available because this App Service was created on the standard pricing tier. If you created yours on the free tier, private endpoints will be grayed out. Let's click this, and here we can create the private endpoint. I'll click Add and select the VNet where I want the private endpoint created and the subnet.

Then I just need to give this a name because it will get created as a separate resource. It'll take a minute or so to create this, and you can watch the status from the

Notifications tab at the top. Once it's created, we could navigate to the resource from here, but let's go to the VNet where it was created. That was vnet1. Under Connected devices, you can see there's the network interface for the virtual machine that was added earlier, and here's the network interface for the App Service.

And you can see they both have private IP addresses from the VNet, and they're part of the web subnet. So that's how you can create a private endpoint for an App Service. In summary, you learned about networking in Azure, starting with an overview. Then you saw how to configure some of the main services, first virtual networks and subnets, then network security groups. After that, you saw how to peer virtual networks in Azure, and then you learned about the ways to connect your on-premises network to Azure using VPN Gateway and ExpressRoute. Then we talked about Azure DNS and how to configure private endpoints to services in Azure. Next, we're going to look at data storage options in Azure.

Chapter 37 Azure Data Storage Options

Modern applications require data to be available quickly and securely from all over the world, and users expect to be able to access, share, and update their data from different devices at any time. Organizations are creating more data than ever, so storing data in the cloud requires addressing new problems in a flexible way, as well as solving old problems in new ways. Azure provides a variety of cloud storage services for different types of data that allows you to choose the storage service that's best optimized for your data and to include several strategies in the same solution, if needed. But common to all the storage solutions in Azure are important benefits like automated backup and recovery, replication across the world to protect your data against unplanned events and failures, encryption capabilities, and built-in security through things like integration with Azure Active Directory for authentication, and developer packages, libraries, and well-documented APIs that can make data accessible to a variety of application types and platforms. Data generally falls into one of three general categories. Structured data is data that adheres to a schema, usually data stored in a database with rows and columns. It's generally referred to as relational data. Azure lets you host databases on virtual machines just like you would on-premises where you're responsible for managing and patching the database product, but Azure also has managed offerings which provide convenience and scalability. For SQL Server, there is Azure SQL Database, and there is also Azure Database for MySQL and Azure Database for PostgreSQL, which are all managed Platform as a Service offerings. Unstructured data is data that doesn't adhere to a schema and is usually data stored in different file formats, so PDF documents, JPEG images, video files and JSON files. For that data, Azure Storage provides highly scalable solutions with Azure Blob storage and Azure File storage. File storage can be attached to virtual machines using the SMB protocol, similar to on-premises file shares, but both types of storage also offer REST APIs, so data can be securely accessed over the internet. Azure Storage also stores large files like disk images and SQL databases. Semi-structured data doesn't fit neatly into tables, rows, and columns. It's often called NoSQL or non-relational data, and it usually uses tags or keys that organize the data and provide a hierarchy. For this type of data, Azure offers Cosmos DB, which is a globally distributed service to store data that's constantly being updated by users around the world. Being able to provision these different types of storage solutions quickly and in a cost effective way helps you respond to business change without the need to procure and manage the costly storage media and networking components required to connect it all together. This makes data storage a very strong value proposition for moving to Azure. We'll be looking at Azure Storage accounts. This is the focus of the data storage portion of the AZ-900 exam. We'll look at redundancy options for storage accounts, so making copies of your data in different locations. We'll create a storage account and explore the features of blobs and files in Azure Storage. Then you'll learn about some of the options for transferring data into Azure using online methods with tools like Azure Storage Explorer and a command-line utility called AzCopy. And for transferring larger amounts of data, there is a service called Azure Data Box where Microsoft will send you hard drives for you to copy your data onto and send back to be copied into Azure. We'll discuss migrating other types of workloads to Azure also, like servers and applications using a service called Azure Migrate. Let's get started by looking at Azure Storage.

Chapter 38 Azure Storage Accounts

Azure Storage is a set of services in Azure that provides storage for a variety of data types using a few different services. Those services are managed under an Azure Storage account. The Blob storage service is for unstructured data like files and documents. Then there is File storage that's similar to Blob storage, except that it supports the SMB protocol, so it can be attached to virtual machines like a network drive, and this makes migrating traditional on-premises applications to the cloud much easier. There is Disk storage which stores the virtual machine disks used by Infrastructure as a Service VMs. There is the Table storage service that lets you store structured data in the form of NoSQL non-relational data, similar to the data you can store using Cosmos DB. And finally, there is the Queue service that's used to store and retrieve messages to help you build asynchronous reliable applications that pass messages. Let's talk about some of the general features of Azure Storage. Azure Storage is durable and highly available. Your data is stored three times in the primary data center by default, and you can choose other replication options that copy the data automatically to other regions in Azure. Your data in Azure Storage can be reached over HTTPS from the internet and each of the storage services in an Azure Storage account has its own REST endpoint, but of course, you can apply security controls to those endpoints to prevent unauthorized access. Security is a big topic for storage accounts. At a high level, when you want to control access to the data plane of a storage account to allow access to the data, you can provide access using role-based access control for users with identities stored in Azure Active Directory and that works for the blob, file, and table services in your storage account. Or you can provide a storage account key that gives access to the entire storage account. You can also provide a user with something called a shared access signature. A shared access signature is a security token string, and it can scope access to a particular service like only the Blob service, as well as to a particular container or even an individual blob, and it can also scope access to a range of time and a particular set of permissions like only allowing reads or updates or deletes. A shared access signature gets appended to the end of the URL to a blob or file in Azure Storage so you're able to have pretty fine-grained access control to data in Azure Storage using shared access signatures, and data in your storage account is encrypted. You can even use your own encryption keys. Besides accessing your data using the REST endpoints, there are SDKs for a variety of languages like .NET, Java, PHP, and others, as well as support for scripting in PowerShell and the Azure CLI. Microsoft also offers free tools like Azure Storage Explorer, which provides a graphical user interface and a command-line utility called AzCopy to make it easy to move data into and out of your storage account. There are four types of storage accounts, standard general purpose v2 storage accounts support blobs, file shares, queues, and tables. This is the recommended storage account type for most situations. It offers the most redundancy options, meaning you can have copies of your data in other regions. Premium Block Blob storage is for storing blobs only and it's for scenarios when you need high transaction rates and low latency. You're limited to only storing your data within a single Azure region though. Premium file shares are for high performance file storage, but you could only store files with this type of account, and again, you're limited to storage within a single Azure region. Premium page blobs are for storing larger blobs like databases and VMs for disks. You can store these types of files in general purpose v2 storage accounts too, but the premium page blob account type gives you better performance when it's needed. Again, your redundancy options are limited. All of the premium account types use solid-state drives for low latency and high throughput. You can't change the storage account type after it's been created. You would need to create a storage account of a different type and move your data over. Next, let's talk about redundancy options for Azure Storage accounts.

Chapter 39 Azure Storage Account Redundancy Options

Redundancy with Azure Storage is about protecting your data from unplanned events like hardware failures, network outages, and even natural disasters. You do that by making copies of your data, which is called replication. Your data is always replicated in the primary data center, you can just expand that with other options. There are three categories that group the redundancy options: redundancy in the primary region, redundancy in a secondary region, and read access to data in the secondary region. Let's start with the primary region. Locally redundant storage is the lowest cost replication option. Your data is copied three times within a single physical data center. It protects you from failures of a server rack or a disk drive within the data center, but because all the data is within a single data center, there is still the risk of a data center level disaster like a fire or a flood. To help mitigate that risk, the next storage type is zone-redundant storage. This storage replicates your data across three availability zones in a single region. Availability zones are data centers within a region that have their own separate power, cooling, and networking. Zone-redundant storage isn't available in every Azure region. Locally redundant storage and zone-redundant storage provide redundancy in the primary Azure region that your storage account is located in, but in the event of a regional disaster where multiple availability zones are affected, there are other options that allow you to copy your data to another Azure region. Geo-redundant storage copies your data three times in the primary region within a single data center and also copies the data asynchronously to a single location in a secondary region. The data is copied three times in the secondary data center, it's basically locally redundant storage in two regions. The secondary region is decided by Microsoft and you can't change that, but it's selected to be hundreds of miles away from the primary region to prevent data loss in the event of a natural disaster. Microsoft lists the paired regions on their website. The second option for redundancy in a secondary region is geo-zone-redundant storage. This replication option uses zone-redundant storage in the primary data center and locally redundant storage in the secondary data center. With geo-redundant and geo-zone-redundant storage, the data in the secondary region is only available to be read if you or Microsoft initiates a failover from the primary region to the secondary. You might want to always have the ability for your applications to read the data in the secondary region. To enable this, there are two other account types, read-access-geo-redundant storage and read-access-geo-zone-redundant storage. The two options are similar to the previous ones we discussed, geo-redundant and geo-zone-redundant storage. They just add the ability to always be able to read the data from the secondary region. The replication options available depend on which storage account type you select. Let's create a storage account in the Azure portal.

Chapter 40 How to Create a Storage Account

Let's create an Azure Storage account so we can explore some of the features and configuration options. As usual, I'll go to All services and search for storage. Clicking on Storage Accounts brings us to the list of storage accounts in this subscription. We could have also gotten there from the shortcut on the left menu. From here, let's create a new storage account. The first thing we need to do is choose a resource group for the storage account, I have one created already. Then we need to give the storage account a name and this name needs to be unique across all of Azure because it will become part of the URL to each of the storage endpoints for the blob, file, table, and queue services. Now we choose the region. Before I change the default, I just want to show you how the choice of region affects the redundancy options available.

Create a storage account

Basics   Advanced   Networking   Data protection   Encryption   Tags   Review

Azure Storage is a Microsoft-managed service providing cloud storage that is highly available, secure, durable, scalable, and redundant. Azure Storage includes Azure Blobs (objects), Azure Data Lake Storage Gen2, Azure Files, Azure Queues, and Azure Tables. The cost of your storage account depends on the usage and the options you choose below. Learn more about Azure storage accounts

Project details

Select the subscription in which to create the new storage account. Choose a new or existing resource group to organize and manage your storage account together with other resources.

Subscription *   Visual Studio Professional

    Resource group *   storage_rg
                                    Create new

Instance details

If you need to create a legacy storage accou...   Locally-redundant storage (LRS):
                                                    Lowest-cost option with basic protection against server rack and drive
Storage account name * ...   failures. Recommended for non-critical scenarios.

Region ...   Geo-redundant storage (GRS):
                                                    Intermediate option with failover capabilities in a secondary region.
                                                    Recommended for backup scenarios.
Performance ...

                                                    Zone-redundant storage (ZRS):
                                                    Intermediate option with protection against datacenter-level failures.
                                                    Recommended for high availability scenarios.
Redundancy ...
                                                    Geo-redundant storage (GRS)

                                                    ☑ Make read access to data available in the event of regional unavailability.

  Review   < Previous   Next : Advanced >

For the East US region, the options are Locally-redundant, so just in a single region, Geo-redundant, so with failover to a secondary region, and Zone-redundant storage. If I change the region to Canada Central, we have all the same choices plus Geo-zone-redundant storage, so that's not available for all Azure regions, but let's go with Locally-redundant storage, the cheapest option. Next, we choose the storage account type which is labeled as performance. The standard selection is for a general-purpose v2 storage account type, but we can change this to Premium and choose from Block blobs, File shares, or Page blobs.

These account types store data on solid-state drives, but they're limited to just the type of data in the description, so file storage won't let you store blobs, tables, or queues. Each of these options offers better performance and might be suitable depending on your business requirements, but you'll notice that choosing any of these limits the redundancy options to just Locally-redundant storage. Let's change this back to Standard and move to the Advanced tab.

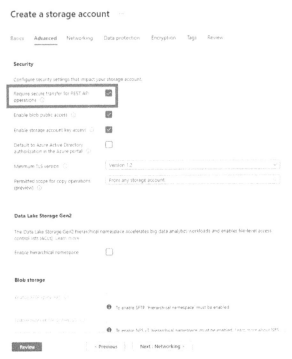

Here, you can choose from some security options like requiring HTTPS on the REST API to the storage account allowing anonymous access to Blob storage, then there is options to Enable hierarchical namespace for the Blob service, which will allow it to be used for Data Lake Storage Gen 2. That adds some security options, and the hierarchical namespace makes it easier to do the type of bulk operations required by big data analysis tools. You can choose the default Access tier when uploading blobs.

Access tiers can have a significant impact on the cost of storing your data, and you can enable large files for Azure File storage.

Normally, file shares are limited to 5 TB in size, but by choosing this option, you can create file shares up to 100 TB. Let's move on to networking.

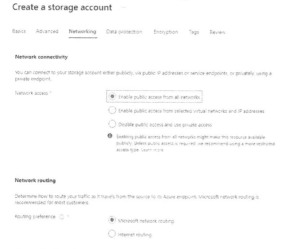

The default is to Enable public access, so this includes the internet and this is for the REST endpoints to all the storage services, which of course, you can secure by requiring the caller to authenticate or you can specify virtual networks within Azure and public IP addresses on the internet that you want to restrict access to. And you can also select to only have the storage account available over a private endpoint. Let's use the default and move on to data protection. You have the ability to Enable soft delete for blobs, containers, which hold blobs, and for file shares.

This essentially gives you a recycle bin where you can recover deleted files and folders. Then there are some options for versioning of blobs and enabling the change feed to record when blobs are created, modified, and deleted. Let's move on to encryption. The data in your storage account is encrypted by default, but you might have a need to manage your own encryption keys, maybe for regulatory compliance. You can do that using an encryption key that you　　　store　　　in　　　Azure　　　Key　　　Vault.

We haven't talked about Key Vault, but it's a central service in Azure to securely store secrets like encryption keys, SSL certificates for web apps, and strings, like database connection strings. They can all be managed in one place and accessed by applications that have permissions. Let's leave the default and let's go to Tags. We won't create any tags. So let's review the configuration and create this storage account.

Once the storage account is created, we can navigate to it by going to all storage accounts and there is the new storage account we created. Before we explore the storage account, let's talk about blob access tiers next.

Chapter 41 Azure Blobs and Access Tiers

Now let's talk about blobs and how you can save on storage costs by using a feature called blob access tiers. BLOB is an acronym for binary large object. A blob can be any type of file, including documents, video files, text files, even virtual machine disks. The Blob service is optimized for storing massive amounts of unstructured data, and by unstructured data, I mean data that doesn't adhere to a particular data model or definition. There are three types of blobs you can store: block blobs, stored text, and binary data. They're called block blobs because a single blob is made up of multiple blocks and that helps you optimize uploading. Append blobs are made up of blocks also, but they're optimized for appending only, so they're a good choice for logs where you only add to the file. And page blobs store random access files up to 8 TB in size, so they're used to store disks for virtual machines and databases. Page blobs are made up of 512-byte pages and are designed for frequent random read/write applications, so they're the foundation of Azure Disks. Block Blob storage is the most cost effective way to store a large number of files, and one of the features that helps you save is blob access tiers The cost of Azure storage comes from the amount of storage, as well as transaction costs related to accessing the data. So there are three blob access tiers that you can choose from to tailor these costs to the way that you use your data. The hot access tier is for data that's accessed frequently so it has the highest storage cost, but the lowest transaction costs. Cool storage is for storing data that you don't access frequently, so the storage cost is lower, but the transaction cost is higher when compared to the hot access tier. And the archive access tier is for storing data that you rarely access.

It's very inexpensive to store a large amount of data, but you have to be willing to wait hours to rehydrate the data if you do need to access it, but for organizations that have requirements to archive large amounts of data, there can be big cost savings by using the archive tier. With some data, the need to access it drops as the data ages, so Blob storage also has a feature called lifecycle management, which lets you set policies to move blobs between access tiers so you can design policies that provide the least expensive storage for your needs without having to manually move the data around. Blob storage has a lot of other features too, like creating snapshots of blobs, leasing blobs to prevent other people from modifying them. You can enable soft delete to essentially provide a recycle bin for your blobs, and you can even host static websites directly in Blob storage so you don't have to host simple HTML and JavaScript sites in Azure App service or on a virtual machine. Blob storage also integrates with other Azure services like the content delivery network, so you can optimize the delivery of blobs to clients all over the world. Azure Search integrates with Blob storage too so you can index the contents of blobs, which enables searching inside the contents of the documents like Word docs, PDFs, Excel spreadsheets, PowerPoint files, and lots of other types. So the Blob service and Azure Storage accounts can be an integral part of applications that use unstructured data. Let's talk about File storage next.

Chapter 42 Azure File Attachments

You can attach File storage to virtual machines to act like network drives. The file share will show up as a drive letter in the virtual machine, just like on-premises storage. When you're moving applications from on-premises to the cloud, there is inevitably going to be some applications that rely on data or configuration being stored on a file share. With the SMB support that Azure Files brings, you can migrate those apps much easier. Something that distinguishes Azure file storage from traditional file shares is that you can make the files accessible from anywhere in the world using a URL to the file with a shared access signature appended on the end. Azure file shares can be mounted concurrently by cloud or on-premises deployments of Windows, Linux, and macOS. In order to map an Azure file share to on-premises using the SMB protocol, you need to open port 445, which is used by SMB. If your organization requires that port 445 be blocked, you can use Azure VPN Gateway or ExpressRoute to tunnel traffic. You'll need to set up a private endpoint for your storage account to do that though. Moreover, Azure File shares can be cached on Windows Servers with Azure File Sync. That provides you fast access near where the data is being used. It actually allows you to tier files based on how they're used. You can keep recently accessed files on your on-premises servers while seamlessly moving old and files that aren't used as frequently to Azure. This helps you manage unpredictable storage growth, and essentially turns your on-premises file server into a quick cache of your Azure file share. You do that by installing a sync agent on the local server. Azure Files has different storage tiers. There are premium file shares, which are part of the File Storage storage account type. We talked about storage account types in the overview on Azure Storage accounts. Premium file shares run on solid-state drives so you get high performance and low latency, so single-digit milliseconds for most input/output operations. Transaction optimized file shares are backed by hard disk drives, and therefore, transaction heavy workloads that don't require the low latency of the premium tier. These are good for applications that require File storage as a back-end store. Hot file shares are for general-purpose file sharing, like team shares, and it works well as the storage for Azure File Sync also. Cool file shares offer the most cost-efficient storage for offline archive storage. Hot and cool file shares are similar to the access tiers that you learned about for Blob storage. You choose the storage tier when you create the file share, but with the tiers on the general-purpose v2 storage account type, you can change the storage tier after the file share has been created. So next, let's explore the storage account that we created earlier and upload some data.

Chapter 43 How to Explore Azure Storage Accounts

Let's explore some of the features of the Blob and File services in the Azure Storage account that we created earlier. From the list of all storage accounts, I'll open that one. From the menu on the left, you can access each of the services in this general purpose v2 storage account.

Containers are the Blob service, File shares are the File service, and the Queue and Table services. Below those are general settings for the storage account. Let's look at blob containers. Containers are the logical groupings of blobs. You can think of them like folders, but they're really just a path in the URL to the file. Let's create a new container. I'll just give it a name and you can specify an access level.

This means that you can require everyone accessing blobs in this container to authenticate, which is the private option, or you can allow anonymous read access to just the blobs and not to be able to list the container contents or the container option allows anonymous access to both the blobs and the container. Let's leave this as private and create the container. I'll navigate into the container and it's empty, so let's upload some data. I'll go to my desktop and there are some files in this folder. I'll select them all and click Open. Under Advanced, we can specify the blob type, and we can also specify the access tier.

So if this data is meant to be archived, we can send it right to the archive tier during the upload. We can also specify a folder, which is similar to the container in that it's just part of the path in the URL. Once the upload is complete, I'll close this window and let's click on one of these files. So this just opens the metadata about the file, not the file itself. From here, we can change the access tier of this blob. On the right side, there is a pop-up menu for each blob.

Blob type	Size	Lease state
Block blob	34.51 KiB	
Block blob	2.42 MiB	
Block blob	7.4 MiB	

- View/edit
- Download
- Properties
- Generate SAS
- View versions
- View snapshots
- Create snapshot
- Change tier
- Acquire lease
- Delete

This is where you can download the file or create a snapshot so a version of the file. You can acquire a lease to prevent other users from modifying the file and you can generate a shared access signature. Let's click that. This lets us choose the parameters for the token, like the permissions we want to give, how long it's valid for, and the IP addresses the user must be coming from in order to access this blob.

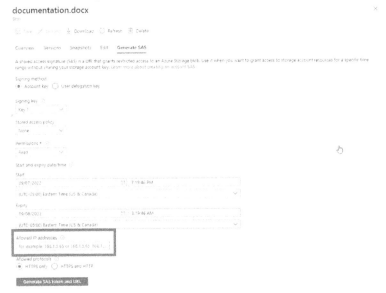

Let's generate this with the defaults. That gives us a URL to the blob with the shared access signature token appended on the end, but let's close out of the container and go back to the Storage Account menu. Now let's go to File shares and let's create a file share.

You need to give the file share a name and then you can choose the storage tier. Premium isn't available because the storage account was created with a general purpose v2 storage account type, but you can choose between Transaction optimized, Hot, and Cool storage tiers. Let's create this file share. And once it's created, I'll click to open it. From here, we can upload files and change the storage tier. We can also generate a script to run on a virtual machine in Azure, then it will show up on the VM with a drive letter. We can do that for Windows, Linux, and macOS because remember, it's also possible to connect to this file share from on-premises. Let's close out of this and let's go back to the root of the storage account. I want to show you some of the configuration options here. Under configuration, you can change some of the settings we chose when setting up the storage account like the default Blob access tier and the Replication option.

We could change this to Geo-redundant storage. Farther up the menu, there are a number of options under Security and networking. You can create a shared access signature to allow access to the services within the storage account, so this provides more access than the token we generated to the individual blob, and you could also provide the access key to the entire storage account.

This isn't recommended though because it provides full control of the storage account. You can rotate the primary and backup keys here which would remove that access, and the shared access signatures are actually generated using these keys too, so if you wanted to revoke the shared access signatures before they expire, you could just rotate the keys here. On the Networking tab, you can disable access from the internet and you might do this if you set up a private endpoint or you can enable access from your virtual networks.

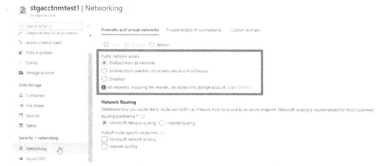

On the Azure CDN tab, you can integrate the storage account with the Azure Content Delivery Network, which would cache the data in locations around the world for faster access times. We won't go into the Azure CDN here, but it can really increase speed and availability of files to users in locations outside the region where the storage account is located.

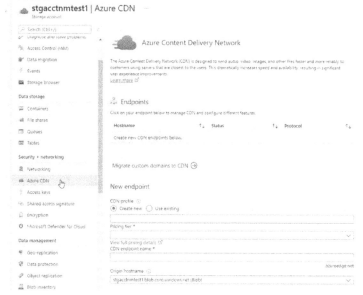

Farther down the menu, there is an option for Static website. This allows you to host static HTML pages and client-side scripts.

This is less expensive than hosting a full app service when all you need is a website without any server-side processing or frameworks installed. Azure Search lets you integrate your storage account with the Azure Search service so your blobs can be indexed and searchable, that includes being able to search the contents of a variety of file types like Word documents and PDFs.

You need to create a search service in order to do that though. We won't go into Azure Search in this book. When you want to access a blob in the Blob service, it would be at this endpoint, followed by the container name and the blob name. Uploading files manually using the Azure portal can be quite time-consuming, so in the next chapter, let's look at other ways to manage files in Azure.

Chapter 44 Azure Data Transfer Options

Let's talk about some of the options for moving data into Azure Storage. The approach you choose depends on a few factors, the amount of data you need to transfer, the frequency, meaning is this a one-time transfer or will you be periodically pushing data into the Azure Storage account, and the last factor is network bandwidth. If you've got a slow connection, transferring large amounts of data can take quite a while. Even if you have a larger connection, you might not want to use up all the network bandwidth for data transfer. For smaller amounts of data, so I'm talking about gigabytes or terabytes of data, if you've got a decent network connection, there are a few tools available. Of course, you can use the Azure portal to upload data to Azure Storage like you saw it earlier, but there is also Azure Storage Explorer, which offers a graphical user interface and makes moving data as easy as using File Explorer, so it's a good choice if you need to delegate some tasks to business users, but it also offers management capabilities for a storage account so it can be used by administrators too. Behind the scenes, Azure Storage Explorer uses a tool called AzCopy. It's actually a command line tool that you can use directly. AzCopy provides features for uploading in a very performant way by leveraging multiple connections at once, and you can integrate AzCopy commands into your scripting activities to copy data to and from Azure. PowerShell and the Azure command line interface also have commands for managing data in Azure. For developers, there are also the client SDKs available in a variety of languages, so you can integrate data ingestion to Azure Storage as part of application development. Earlier, I mentioned Azure File Sync as a way to extend your on-premises file shares to Azure. This way, data that you access frequently is kept on-premises, and data that you use less often is automatically stored in Azure. Azure File Sync is always online, and you don't need to manually move the data to Azure. These are some of the ways that you can get data into Azure using a connection over the internet. Sometimes that's not convenient or even possible due to the amount of data or the throughput of your internet connection. So we'll talk about some options for offline data transfer later, but first, let's take a look at Azure Storage Explorer and AzCopy.

Chapter 45 Azure Storage Explorer

Now let's talk about a tool for managing the data in your Azure Storage account. Azure Storage Explorer is a tool that you can download for Windows, Mac, and Linux and it runs on your local desktop. I've already installed it on my local computer, so let's search for it and open it up.

We need to log into Azure, so let's add an account. There are a number of ways to authenticate. You can log into the whole Azure subscription so the administrator would likely do this, or you can scope the login to just the resource the user needs access to like a blob container or a file share. This is great if you want to give access to an end user to upload files to Azure Storage. You don't want them to have any more access than they need so you set the permissions in Azure Storage and have them log into the resource that they need access to.

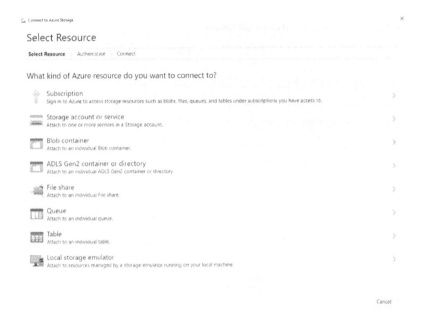

Select Resource

Select Resource   Authenticate   Connect

What kind of Azure resource do you want to connect to?

Subscription
Sign in to Azure to access storage resources such as blobs, files, queues, and tables under subscriptions you have access to.   >

Storage account or service
Attach to one or more services in a Storage account.   >

Blob container
Attach to an individual Blob container.   >

ADLS Gen2 container or directory
Attach to an individual ADLS Gen2 container or directory.   >

File share
Attach to an individual File share.   >

Queue
Attach to an individual queue.   >

Table
Attach to an individual table.   >

Local storage emulator
Attach to resources managed by a storage emulator running on your local machine.   >

Cancel

Let's use the subscription option and hit Next. That opens a browser and I'll select my administrator account, enter my password, and I have multifactor authentication enabled so I need to send a code to my phone and then enter that. Now I'm logged in and my account shows here along with the subscriptions that I have access to.

I'll go to the Explorer tab and expand the subscription. All the storage accounts are listed and below that are disks. This is a big advantage to using Storage Explorer. You can manage the disks used by virtual machines in your subscription, and I'll show you that shortly. First, let's expand the storage account we created earlier. If I right-click on that storage account, I have some options to manage it like copying the access keys and setting the default blob access tier. Let's expand the Blob service and click on this container.

The blobs show on the left, and by right-clicking on the container, I can do things like copy the container, get a shared access signature to provide someone else access to the container, and set the public access level.

You can manage the blobs in the container from here also. Right-clicking, you can change the blob access tier for the individual blob. You can acquire a lease, create a snapshot, and edit tags.

Of course, you can upload blobs from here also with the same options you saw in the portal like setting the access tier. Let's cancel out and look at file shares. From here, you can create file shares and upload and download data, and you can get the script to attach this file share to a Windows VM, but let's close this and look at the Tables service. There are some tables here because classic metrics are enabled on this storage account. In the second table here, there is some data, and you can run queries against this data from here if you like.

With the Queues service, you can create a new queue, so this might be for applications or components that need to pass messages. And you can create queue messages from here also, which you might want to do for testing during development.

Let's close this storage account and now let's look at disks. I have this resource group that's storing the operating system disk for the VM that I created earlier. From here, you can download the disk image and also create a snapshot, and you can also upload disk images from on-premises to Azure.

You select the operating system type, you can select whether it should be stored on a solid-state drive or a hard drive, and the generation of the Hyper-V image.

Azure Storage Explorer gives you a graphical user interface that lets you do some management of your Azure Storage account, and it's great for transferring data to and from Azure. It also lets you delegate access to other people with an easy-to-use interface. Azure Storage Explorer actually uses a utility called AzCopy to transfer the files, and you can use AzCopy directly too, so let's look at that next.

Chapter 46 How to Use AzCopy to Upload & Manage Blobs

Let's take a look at the AzCopy command line utility. You can download it from docs.microsoft.com, and it's available for Windows, Mac, and Linux. I've already downloaded it, and you just need to unzip it and navigate to the folder where it's stored, it doesn't get installed. I've copied it to the root of my C drive. So I'll open up the Windows command prompt and I'll change directories to the root of the C drive where the AzCopy file is stored. We need to authenticate to Azure, so I'll type azcopy login.

It says I need to open up a browser and go to microsoft.com/devicelogin and paste in this code, so let's do that. And I'll paste in the code I copied and select my administrator account and just click Continue to log in. Now we can run some commands, but before we do that, I need to show you something in the Azure portal. I'll navigate into the storage account that we're going to be working against with AzCopy. Let's go to Access Control and view my access. I had to give my administrator account this permission called Storage Blob Data Contributor.

That will give the account access to create and modify blobs in the storage account. You don't actually have to log in using Azure AD. You can just attach a shared access signature on all of your calls with AzCopy, but using the Azure AD login is just more convenient. Let's open up the Containers tab and now go back to the command prompt and run some commands. Azcopy make will create the container name at the end of the URL to the Blob service in my storage account.

```
C:\>azcopy make "https://stgacctnmtest1.blob.core.windows.net/azcopycontainer"
```

It says it's being created, so let's go to the portal and refresh the list, and there is the new container. Let's open it up. And now let's upload some files back in the command prompt. I have these files on my local computer. Let's copy the DOCX file. You do that with the azcopy command specifying the source and destination.

```
C:\>azcopy copy "C:\Users\neilm\Desktop\files\documentation.docx" "https://stgacctnmtest1.blob.core.windows.net/azcopycontainer/newname.docx"
```

The source can be a local file or folder or even a container in another storage account, and you can change the name of the file in the destination, so it's the same file just with a different name. It shows that it was successful, so let's go to the portal and refresh the container, and there is the file with the new name. The last thing I want to do is to use AzCopy to change the access tier of one of these files. I want to change it from hot to cool because I know I won't need to access this file, and I'd like to save on storage costs. So back at the command prompt, I'll use azcopy set-properties with a path to the file and the parameter block-blob-tier set to cool.

```
C:\>azcopy set-properties "https://stgacctnmtest1.blob.core.windows.net/azcopycontainer/newname.docx" --block-blob-tier=cool
INFO: Authenticating to source using Azure AD
INFO: Any empty folders will not be processed, because source and/or destination doesn't have full folder support

Job f7840443-f2cd-944a-6101-c266b6bbe81a has started
Log file is located at: C:\Users\neilm\.azcopy\f7840443-f2cd-944a-6101-c266b6bbe81a.log

INFO: Transfers are likely to fail because destination does not support tiers.
0.0 %, 1 Done, 0 Failed, 0 Pending, 0 Skipped, 1 Total,


Job f7840443-f2cd-944a-6101-c266b6bbe81a summary
Elapsed Time (Minutes): 0.0335
Number of File Transfers: 1
Number of Folder Property Transfers: 0
Total Number of Transfers: 1
Number of Transfers Completed: 1
Number of Transfers Failed: 0
Number of Transfers Skipped: 0
TotalBytesTransferred: 0
Final Job Status: Completed
```

No failures, so let's take a look in the portal. And the blob access tier has been changed.

Modified	Access tier	Archive status	Blob type	Size	Lease state
9/7/2022 8:36:26 PM	Cool		Block blob	34.51 KiB	Available
6/7/2022 8:37:17 PM	Hot (inferred)		Block blob	2.42 MiB	Available

AzCopy is a powerful tool that you can use for managing files in Azure and you can use when creating scripts for batch jobs. Next, let's talk about managed database products in Azure.

Chapter 47 Managed Database Products in Azure

Azure offers managed database solutions for storing structured data in relational databases. Let's start by talking about Microsoft's own relational database management system, SQL Server. There are three offerings for SQL Server in Azure that make up the SQL Server family of products. You can host SQL Server on virtual machines, which gives you full control over the product and all the features you're accustomed to hosting SQL Server in your own on-premises data center, but you can also provision a virtual machine with SQL Server already installed by using the Azure Marketplace, and you can take advantage of pay-as-you-go pricing so you don't have the costly upfront licensing fees. You even have the ability to configure a maintenance window for some automated patching, and you can configure backups using a managed backup service in Azure. Then there is a fully-managed platform-as-a-service version of SQL Server called Azure SQL Database. Most database management functions are handled for you like upgrading, patching, backups, and monitoring. Azure SQL Database is always running the latest stable version of SQL Server with high availability guarantees. There is also flexible pricing models based on either the number of virtual cores or using a unit of measurement called DTUs, which stands for database transaction units, and makes up a combination of CPU, memory, and data throughput. Azure SQL database also has flexible deployment options. You can provision a single isolated database or what's called an elastic pool, which is a collection of databases with a shared set of resources. With single databases, you can still harness the elasticity of the cloud by scaling database resources up and down when needed. There are different service tiers available too like the standard tier for common workloads, the business critical premium tier for applications with high transaction rates, and the hyperscale tier for very large transactional databases. Running SQL Server on a virtual machine, you get access to all the features of the product so there are some limitations to using Azure SQL Database. The majority of core features are available in the managed version, but if you have some specific requirements, you can verify compatibility with Azure SQL Database in the Microsoft documentation. If you have compatibility concerns, there is also a third offering called Azure SQL Managed Instance. It combines the broadest set of SQL Server capabilities with the benefits of a fully-managed platform. It allows you to deploy a managed VM with SQL Server onto your own virtual network. Some organizations have security concerns about deploying databases onto a managed public cloud platform, so SQL Server Managed Instance lets you lift and shift your on-premises databases to the cloud with minimal changes and into an isolated environment with the networking controls while also getting the advantages of automatic patching and version updates, automated backups, and high availability. Those are some of the options for using SQL Server in Azure, but there are other database options available in Azure. Using the Azure Marketplace, you can provision a variety of virtual machines with various relational database systems preinstalled, but of course, you'll be managing those servers and databases yourself. In terms of fully-managed platform-as-a-service offerings, Azure offers Azure Database for my SQL and Azure Database for PostgreSQL. These are hosted versions with pay-as-you-go pricing, and you get high availability and automated patching of the underlying database engine. Next, let's talk about how you can migrate different types of workloads, including SQL Server from your on-premises environment into Azure.

Chapter 48 Azure Migrate Fundamentals

Azure Migrate is a unified migration platform that allows you to start, run, and track your migrations to Azure. It lets you assess your on-premises infrastructure, data, and platforms to determine how to migrate them to Azure. Azure Migrate can assess your on-premises physical and virtual servers for migrating them to Azure virtual machines. It can assess on-premises SQL Server instances to migrate them to SQL running on a VM, an Azure SQL Database, or an Azure SQL Managed Instance. It can assess web applications running on-premises and migrate them to run on Azure App service or the Azure Kubernetes service. For migrating large amounts of unstructured data offline, Databox is a service that's part of Azure Migrate. You can track your data migrations in the Azure Migrate portal, and you can also assess your on-premises virtual desktop infrastructure and migrate it to Azure Virtual Desktop. Azure Migrate is made up of several tools, let's look at some of them. Let's start with migrating servers. The Azure Migrate: Discovery and Assessment tool looks at physical servers hosted on-premises and virtual machines running on Hyper-V and VMware. It assesses whether the VMs are ready for migration to Azure, including the web apps and SQL servers running on the VMs. The tool estimates the size of the virtual machine that will be needed in Azure and estimates the costs for running the servers that you need. The tool also identifies cross-server dependencies and makes recommendations for optimization. You download a virtual appliance to your environment to do the assessment, and it can run on a physical or virtual server. It discovers on-premises servers and sends metadata and performance data to Azure Migrate. Then you can use the Azure Migrate

Server Migration tool to actually replicate your on-premises servers into Azure. You can also migrate servers hosted in other cloud environments. You download and install a replication appliance in your environment and install the mobility service agent on the servers you want to replicate to Azure, Then you can replicate up to 10 servers at once and track the progress in the Azure Migrate portal. The server migration tool also attracts incremental changes to the on-premises disks after the initial replication and makes updates to the disks in Azure. For migrating on-premises SQL Server databases, there is the Data Migration Assistant and Azure Data Migration service. The migration assistant detects compatibility issues that can impact functionality when migrating to newer versions of SQL Server in the cloud or to Azure SQL Database. It can also recommend performance and reliability improvements. For smaller databases, the migration assistant can move the schema data and objects from your source server to your target database in Azure. The Azure Database Migration service is for large migrations in terms of the number of databases and the size of those databases. Both of the tools can move your SQL Server databases to SQL Server hosted on virtual machines, Azure SQL Database, or Azure SQL Managed Instances. Azure Migrate also has tools to assess and migrate.NET and Java web applications hosted on-premises. They can be moved to Azure App Service as containers or as code. You can also use the Azure Migrate App Containerization tool to containerize existing ASP.NET and Java applications and move them to the Azure Kubernetes service. A Docker file gets created and the container is pushed to the Azure Container Registry for deployment to Kubernetes. The process doesn't even require access to your code base. So next, let's take a look at Azure Migrate in the Azure portal.

Chapter 49 How to Use Azure Migrate to Move Apps to Azure

I'll go to All services and search for migrate. This isn't a service that you create, it's a portal inside the Azure portal to organize all your migration projects.

The different migration options are listed on the left menu. Let's go to Servers. I've already created a project, so the instructions for assessment and migration are listed here. Let's click on Discover.

It asks if the servers we want to migrate are virtual or physical, and notice that physical includes servers hosted on other cloud platforms like Amazon or Google. Let's select

Hyper-V. The next screen is where you can download the appliance to your environment that will do the discovery and assessment.

We won't do this. Let's close out of this and let's see what's involved in creating a new project. There is only a few things you need to enter here, the resource group, give the project a name, and you need to select a geography.

Notice this isn't an Azure region. You learned earlier that geography is organized groups of Azure regions. Under Advanced, you can select whether the migration will be over the public internet or a private endpoint. That's all you need to create a project. Let's close out of this though and let's look at another type of project for migrating web apps. I'll create a new project here, and this looks exactly like the servers project, but let's go ahead and create this. I'll use an existing resource group and enter a project name. Now I'll select my Azure geography, and I'll leave the public endpoint.

The project gets created and the steps here are different than for the server project. It says to download the App Service Migration Assistant.

Let's click this link. That brings us to the overview page for the tool. Scroll down and the tool is available here.

Let's download this. I just have to accept the license terms and an MSI gets downloaded to my local computer. Clicking on the file actually runs the installer, although there is no wizard here to step through. So when this is done, I'll minimize this window and there has been a shortcut installed on my desktop. I'll click this to open up the tool. So I have a web server installed on this Windows 10 computer, Internet Information Services, or IIS, is running the same web server that you would install on a production server in your environment. So the tool detects that and scans the web server. There is only the default site running which is just a web page actually, but it did discover the site so let's proceed with this.

Once the assessment report is complete, it shows all the things that were scanned and it passed all the checks. Next, I'm told to log into Azure. I'll click this and paste in the code that was copied to the clipboard. I need to choose an account, and I'll skip filming all the login stuff because I have multifactor authentication enabled. And once I'm logged in, it asks if I'm trying to sign into the App Service Migration Assistant.

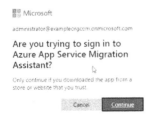

So let's continue and go back to the assistant. Now we can select a project in Azure Migrate. I have several. Let's choose the one I just created. Next, we enter the target in Azure. I'll choose an existing resource group and give this app service a name, which remember, needs to be unique across Azure.

I'll choose an existing app service plan and that's it, let's hit Migrate. And while this is creating the app service in Azure and migrating the code, you can export the Azure Resource Manager template for this app service configuration.

Once the migration is complete, you can navigate to the website deployed in Azure.

This is just a default web page that gets installed locally with IIS, but it shows that the files were successfully copied into Azure App service. So Azure Migrate makes it pretty easy to move resources from on-premises and other cloud providers into Azure. Next, let's talk about Azure Data Box for moving large amounts of data into Azure.

Chapter 50 How to Migrate Data with Azure Data Box

Azure Data Box is a service where Microsoft will ship you a secure device that you copy data onto and send back to Microsoft to load into at Azure. Data Box is actually part of Azure Migrate. So let's go to the Azure Migrate portal and go down to Data Box on the menu.

You select a resource group for the order, then a source country or region, and a destination. Click Apply and the options are here.

There are three tiers to the service depending on how much data you need to transfer. The standard Data Box service is a secure device that can move up to 80 TB of data. It gets transported to you and you copy your data onto the device and ship it back to Microsoft. Or you can use it to export your data from Azure and copy onto your local network. You might use this to move some virtual machines or databases to Azure in a one-time migration. Keep in mind, this isn't just a hard drive that Microsoft is shipping you. These are pictures of the device from the documentation.

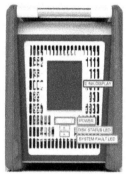 

Data Box front view (left) and back view (right)

It's a rugged device with fast transfer speeds and multiple layers of security and encryption. You can track the status of the transfer right in the Azure portal. For smaller transfers, Azure Data Box Disk can be used. Microsoft can ship you 1 to 5 solid-state disk drives that can hold up to 35 TB of data. The process is the same, and one of the advantages is that it can use USB 3.0 to copy the data locally, so you don't need a network interface like you do with the standard Data Box. You might use this to send backups to Azure Backup without having to transfer them over the network or to seed files in Azure File Sync. On the other end of the spectrum, if you need to transfer more data than the standard Data Box service, you can go with Azure Data Box Heavy. This is a device with 800 TB storage capacity, and it uses a high-performance 40 Gbps network interface. You might use this to move your virtual machine farm or SQL Servers to Azure in a lift and shift type scenario. There is another service available for Microsoft for drive shipping also called the Import/Export service. This allows you to ship your own disk drives to Microsoft to load the data into Azure Blob or File storage. You can also ship disks to Microsoft and have them load your blob data onto the disks to be shipped back to you. There is another product with Azure Data Box and it moves data online so it's not storage that you ship back and forth to Azure. Azure Data Box Gateway is a virtual device hosted in your on-premises environment. You write data to the device like using a file share and then as the data is written to the gateway device, the device uploads the data to Azure Storage. You might still use Data Box for the initial offline transfer and then use Data Box Gateway for incremental ongoing transfers over the network. In summary, you learned about storage options in Azure. We went into depth on storage accounts and their configuration options. We created a storage account and explored blobs and files. You learned about data migration options like using Azure Storage Explorer to upload small amounts of data and Azure Data Box for transferring large amounts of data offline. You also learned about using Azure Migrate to move different types of workloads to Azure. Next, we'll look at ways to manage Azure other than using the Azure portal, as well as monitoring tools in Azure to ensure the health and performance of your resources.

Chapter 51 Azure Resource Manager Basics

So far, we've been creating resources in Azure using the Azure portal. That's a pretty intuitive way to do it, but there are also several tools for managing Azure from the command line and using infrastructure as code. Central to all of Azure Management is Azure Resource Manager, which goes by the acronym ARM. ARM is the deployment and management service for Azure and it's central to all the creation, deletion, and modification of resources that you do in Azure. When you're using the Azure portal, you're really just using a website that sends requests to the ARM endpoint. ARM handles authentication using Azure Active Directory and authorizes that you can perform the action that you're attempting to perform. ARM then sends the request to the Azure Service that you're attempting to create or manipulate. That could be an app service, a virtual machine, an Azure SQL Database, a machine learning workspace, anything in Azure that's a resource, which is basically everything in Azure. ARM is used by all the tools that you use to manage Azure. The Azure portal is an obvious tool, but you can also use PowerShell to create and manage resources in Azure. It's actually done through a set of cmdlets that you install as the Azure PowerShell module. PowerShell works from a Windows, macOS, or Linux computer, and with PowerShell, you can write scripts to automate a series of tasks, so it's really powerful. There is also the Azure command-line interface, or Azure CLI. The Azure CLI is a set of commands used to create and manage Azure resources and it's also available for Windows, macOS, and Linux. It runs in the Windows command prompt on Windows or the Bash Shell on Linux. You can download and install PowerShell or the Azure CLI onto your local workstation, but there is also something called the Cloud Shell in the Azure portal that lets you use these scripting tools right from within the portal in your browser, so you don't need anything installed locally. There is a mobile app for managing Azure that lets you use a graphical user interface on your phone to create and manage Azure resources and receive alerts. There are also SDKs for different programming languages that allow you to call the Azure Resource Manager endpoints so you can build Azure management into a custom solution. Azure Resource Manager was introduced in 2014. Before that, there was the classic deployment model where every resource existed independently. You couldn't group resources together. The concept of resource groups was a major addition that came with ARM. Azure Resource Manager also brought the ability to use Resource Manager templates, which allow you to define your infrastructure using JavaScript Object Notation, or JSON. That lets you deploy infrastructure as code to create the resources for your solutions. And the Azure Resource Manager model also brought the concept of tags which allows you to logically group the resources in your subscription. We're going to look at different ways to manage Azure using the Azure CLI, Azure PowerShell, and we'll see those in the Azure Cloud Shell also. Then you'll learn about Resource Manager templates for deploying infrastructure in a repeatable way. Then I want to show you some of the services in Azure that can help with monitoring and troubleshooting your deployed solutions. Azure Service Health gives you a view of the health of the overall Azure service, so you'll know if there are problems with the platform that could be impacting your applications. Azure Monitor integrates with all the Azure services to provide monitoring of different metrics with alerts you can set up to know when there is an issue. Azure Monitor also contains log analytics which provides extensive logging capabilities that can help with troubleshooting. You'll learn about Microsoft Defender for Cloud which assesses the security of your cloud workloads, provides recommendations, and alerts you to security events. After that, we'll discuss Azure Advisor which provides recommendations for configuration of your deployed resources. Next, you'll see the Azure mobile app, which is a native app for your phone to manage your Azure subscription and receive alerts. Finally, we'll talk about Azure Arc, which lets you monitor resources that are deployed outside of Azure. We've got a lot to get through, so let's start by looking at the Azure CLI next.

Chapter 52 Azure Command Line Interface

The Azure CLI lets you manage Azure resources from the command line. You can download it to your local workstation, and it's available for Windows, Mac, and Linux, and I'll show you later that it's also available right in the Azure portal using the Cloud Shell. All Azure CLI commands start with az, then the command. Before you can use the CLI with your Azure subscription, you need to log in. That's done with the az login command. The first command I'll run is to get the list of resource groups in this subscription. Azure CLI commands are organized into groups and subgroups. Az is actually the parent group, and group is the name of the set of commands for resource groups, then list is the actual command. I'll hit Enter to run this.

```
{
  "id": "/subscriptions/0ef1dba3-743c-4fe2-97bf-8d81c3e64c20/resourceGroups/websitesRG",
  "location": "centralus",
  "managedBy": null,
  "name": "websitesRG",
  "properties": {
    "provisioningState": "Succeeded"
  },
  "tags": null,
  "type": "Microsoft.Resources/resourceGroups"
},
{
  "id": "/subscriptions/0ef1dba3-743c-4fe2-97bf-8d81c3e64c20/resourceGroups/pieshoprg",
  "location": "canadacentral",
  "managedBy": null,
  "name": "pieshoprg",
  "properties": {
    "provisioningState": "Succeeded"
  },
  "tags": null,
  "type": "Microsoft.Resources/resourceGroups"
},
{
  "id": "/subscriptions/0ef1dba3-743c-4fe2-97bf-8d81c3e64c20/resourceGroups/pssamples",
  "location": "eastus2",
  "managedBy": null,
  "name": "pssamples",
  "properties": {
    "provisioningState": "Succeeded"
  },
  "tags": null,
  "type": "Microsoft.Resources/resourceGroups"
}
```

That gives us back a list of the resource groups and their properties, and this is showing a JavaScript Object Notation format, or JSON. Let's run this again, but this time, we'll use a global argument called output, and this lets you format the output of any query. You can modify this to include

208

whatever properties you want, but let's move on. Another useful global argument is help, this will give you information at whatever level you use it. So by typing help after the subgroup name called group, we get a list of all the commands that are available in that subgroup.

```
Group
    az group : Manage resource groups and template deployments.

Subgroups:
    lock     : Manage Azure resource group locks.

Commands:
    create : Create a new resource group.
    delete : Delete a resource group.
    exists : Check if a resource group exists.
    export : Captures a resource group as a template.
    list   : List resource groups.
    show   : Gets a resource group.
    update : Update a resource group.
    wait   : Place the CLI in a waiting state until a condition of the resource group is met.

To search AI knowledge base for examples, use: az find "az group"

Please let us know how we are doing: https://aka.ms/azureclihats
```

There is the list command we used. Let's try using the help argument at the root, the az group. That gives us a list of all the subgroups which have commands for the different services in Azure.

```
ppg                         : Manage Proximity Placement Groups.
private-link                : Private-link association CLI command group.
provider                    : Manage resource providers.
redis                       : Manage dedicated Redis caches for your Azure applications.
relay                       : Manage Azure Relay Service namespaces, WCF relays, hybrid
                              connections, and rules.
reservations    [Preview]   : Manage Azure Reservations.
resource                    : Manage Azure resources.
resourcemanagement          : Resourcemanagement CLI command group.
restore-point               : Manage restore point with res.
role                        : Manage user roles for access control with Azure Active Directory
                              and service principals.
search                      : Manage Azure Search services, admin keys and query keys.
security                    : Manage your security posture with Microsoft Defender for Cloud.
servicebus                  : Manage Azure Service Bus namespaces, queues, topics,
                              subscriptions, rules and geo-disaster recovery configuration
                              alias.
sf                          : Manage and administer Azure Service Fabric clusters.
sig                         : Manage shared image gallery.
signalr                     : Manage Azure SignalR Service.
snapshot                    : Manage point-in-time copies of managed disks, native blobs, or
                              other snapshots.
sql                         : Manage Azure SQL Databases and Data Warehouses.
sshkey                      : Manage ssh public key with vm.
staticwebapp                : Manage static apps.
storage                     : Manage Azure Cloud Storage resources.
synapse         [Preview]   : Manage and operate Synapse Workspace, Spark Pool, SQL
                              Pool.
tag                         : Tag Management on a resource.
term            [Experimental] : Manage marketplace agreement with marketplaceordering.
ts                          : Manage template specs at subscription or resource group scope.
vm                          : Manage Linux or Windows virtual machines.
vmss                        : Manage groupings of virtual machines in an Azure Virtual Machine
                              Scale Set (VMSS).
webapp                      : Manage web apps.
```

There is the appservice subgroup, the Cosmos DB subgroup, the group subgroup that we've been using for resource groups, and there is a subgroup called resource for managing resources. Let's use that one. And we'll list out the resources in a resource group. Let's use the second resource group here. I'll use az resource list, then we need to use some parameters. Resource-group is the name of the group we want it to list the contents of, and let's format the output as a table again. So there is just two resources in this resource group, an app service plan, which is actually called a serverFarm type behind the scenes in Azure, and a site, which is an appservice.

```
Name              ResourceGroup    Location      Type                        Status
-------------     -------------    ----------    ------------------------    -------
pieshopsvcplan    pieshoprg        canadacentral Microsoft.Web/serverFarms
pieshoptesting    pieshoprg        canadacentral Microsoft.Web/sites
```

Now let's create some resources. First, I'll create a resource group using az group create, then the location parameter, and I'll use canadacentral, and the name of this resource group will be cli_rg. The JSON that's returned indicates that it was created successfully.

```
{
  "id": "/subscriptions/0ef1dba3-743c-4fe2-97bf-8d81c3e64c20/resourceGroups/cli_rg",
  "location": "canadacentral",
  "managedBy": null,
  "name": "cli_rg",
  "properties": {
    "provisioningState": "Succeeded"
  },
  "tags": null,
  "type": "Microsoft.Resources/resourceGroups"
}
```

Otherwise, there would be an error showing. Now let's create an appservice, but first we need an app service plan, so I'll use az appservice plan create then the resource group I want it created in, the name I want to call the appservice plan, and we need to provide a sku, which is the code for the pricing tier. I'll use the standard S1 pricing tier, the same one we used when we created an appservice plan earlier in the portal. It'll take a second to provision this, but then the JSON returns to indicate that it worked.

```
"isSpot": false,
"isXenon": false,
"kind": "app",
"kubeEnvironmentProfile": null,
"location": "canadacentral",
"maximumElasticWorkerCount": 1,
"maximumNumberOfWorkers": 0,
"name": "asp-fromcli",
"numberOfSites": 0,
"numberOfWorkers": 1,
"perSiteScaling": false,
"provisioningState": "Succeeded",
"reserved": false,
"resourceGroup": "cli_rg",
"sku": {
  "capabilities": null,
  "capacity": 1,
  "family": "S",
  "locations": null,
  "name": "S1",
  "size": "S1",
  "skuCapacity": null,
  "tier": "Standard"
},
"spotExpirationTime": null,
"status": "Ready",
"subscription": "0ef1dba3-743c-4fe2-97bf-8d81c3e64c20",
"tags": null,
"targetWorkerCount": 0,
"targetWorkerSizeId": 0,
"type": "Microsoft.Web/serverfarms",
"workerTierName": null,
"zoneRedundant": false
```

Now let's create an appservice for the plan. This is actually a different subgroup. We use the create command in the webapp subgroup passing the resource group name, the appservice plan name, and the name of this app service.

```
"scmIpSecurityRestrictionsDefaultAction": null,
"scmIpSecurityRestrictionsUseMain": null,
"scmMinTlsVersion": null,
"scmType": null,
"sitePort": null,
"storageType": null,
"supportedTlsCipherSuites": null,
"tracingOptions": null,
"use32BitWorkerProcess": null,
"virtualApplications": null,
"vnetName": null,
"vnetPrivatePortsCount": null,
"vnetRouteAllEnabled": null,
"webSocketsEnabled": null,
"websiteTimeZone": null,
"winAuthAdminState": null,
"winAuthTenantState": null,
"windowsFxVersion": null,
"xManagedServiceIdentityId": null
},
"slotSwapStatus": null,
"state": "Running",
"storageAccountRequired": false,
"suspendedTill": null,
"tags": null,
"targetSwapSlot": null,
"trafficManagerHostNames": null,
"type": "Microsoft.Web/sites",
"usageState": "Normal",
"virtualNetworkSubnetId": null,
"vnetContentShareEnabled": false,
"vnetImagePullEnabled": false,
"vnetRouteAllEnabled": false
```

It looks like it was created, so let's go to the Azure portal and check. I'll go to Resource groups, and there is the resource group we created using the CLI. It only shows the appservice plan, but sometimes there is just a delay in it showing up in the portal, so I'll hit Refresh, and there is the app service.

Let's click the Browse button and make sure it's working with the default page.

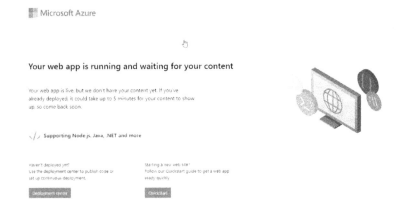

That's how to use the Azure CLI to query and manage resources in Azure. Next, let's look at Azure PowerShell.

Chapter 53 Azure PowerShell

Another way to manage Azure resources is using Azure PowerShell, which is a module for PowerShell that you can install. PowerShell runs on Windows, Mac, and Linux, and Azure PowerShell requires PowerShell version 7 or higher, so you might have to install that first, which is what I had to do on my Windows 10 computer. Then you can install the Azure PowerShell module from right within PowerShell using the install module command. Let's open up PowerShell 7 which runs alongside previous versions of PowerShell. Just like with the Azure CLI, the first thing you need to do is authenticate to Azure. In PowerShell, that's done with connect az account. A browser opens up just like with the CLI allowing us to enter our credentials. I'll use the administrator account in my Azure Active Directory tenant, and I'm already logged in so I don't have to enter the password. Back in PowerShell, it shows that I'm authenticated. Now let's run some commands against Azure. First, let's list the resource groups in the subscription. That's done with Get-AzResourceGroup with no parameters.

```
ResourceGroupName : websitesRG
Location          : centralus
ProvisioningState : Succeeded
Tags              :
ResourceId        : /subscriptions/0ef1dba3-743c-4fe2-97bf-8d81c3e64c20/resourceGroups/websitesRG

ResourceGroupName : pieshoprg
Location          : canadacentral
ProvisioningState : Succeeded
Tags              :
ResourceId        : /subscriptions/0ef1dba3-743c-4fe2-97bf-8d81c3e64c20/resourceGroups/pieshoprg

ResourceGroupName : pssamples
Location          : eastus2
ProvisioningState : Succeeded
Tags              :
ResourceId        : /subscriptions/0ef1dba3-743c-4fe2-97bf-8d81c3e64c20/resourceGroups/pssamples

ResourceGroupName : cli_rg
Location          : canadacentral
ProvisioningState : Succeeded
Tags              :
ResourceId        : /subscriptions/0ef1dba3-743c-4fe2-97bf-8d81c3e64c20/resourceGroups/cli_rg
```

PowerShell commands always start with the action verb so get, in this case. That returns the list, but we can format this in PowerShell too. To do that, you send the output of the first command into another PowerShell command using the pipe operator. So we'll use the Format-Table command with the AutoSize parameter. That's easier to read.

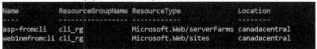

Let's clear this, and now let's list the contents of the resource group we created using the CLI. That's Get-AzResource with the ResourceGroupName parameter, and we'll pipe this to Format-Table. So there is the app service and app service plan we created.

Name	ResourceGroupName	ResourceType	Location
asp-fromcli	cli_rg	Microsoft.Web/serverFarms	canadacentral
web1nmfromcli	cli_rg	Microsoft.Web/sites	canadacentral

Now let's add a storage account to this resource group. First, I'll create a variable to hold the name of the region where I want the storage account created. You can start to see how PowerShell can be used for scripting. Now let's call New-AzStorageAccount passing in the name of the resource group, the name we want to give the storage account, then for the location, we'll use the variable we created. Next is the sku name. I'll use the locally redundant storage option, and finally, the kind of storage account which will be StorageV2.

StorageAccountName	ResourceGroupName	PrimaryLocation	SkuName	Kind	AccessTier	CreationTime	ProvisioningState	EnableHttpsTrafficOnly	LargeFileShares
stgacctnmclitest01	cli_rg	canadacentral	Standard_LRS	StorageV2	Hot	8/31/2022 6:56:09 PM	Succeeded	True	

It shows that the provisioning succeeded, so let's go to the Azure portal and take a look. I'll go to resource groups again and I'll open up the cli_rg, and there are the app service resources.

So using Azure PowerShell or the Azure CLI, you can use commands to manage Azure and also integrate those commands into scripts for more complex operations and deployments, but you do need to install the tools locally. If you're working remotely or don't have permissions to install applications on your local computer, there is an easier way to use the Azure CLI and PowerShell right in the Azure portal using your browser. Let's look at that next.

Chapter 54 How to Use Azure Cloud Shell in Azure Portal

You can run Azure CLI and PowerShell commands right in the Azure portal using the Cloud Shell. Cloud Shell runs on a temporary host container in the background and it requires an Azure file share in an Azure storage account. You only need to create this once, and it will get mounted each time you use the Cloud Shell, so you can persist files that you upload between sessions. You choose either the Bash shell or PowerShell here, but you can change between them any time after this gets created. You can change the options for the storage account creation if you like, the region and resource names, but I'll just leave the defaults.

Let's create the storage account for the Cloud Shell. Once the storage account is created, it'll connect the terminal. You can resize the window, and let's make the text a little bigger from the Settings menu. Let's clear this, and since we're in the Bash shell, it's the clear command. Because I'm already logged into the Azure portal, I don't need to authenticate like I did with the Azure CLI installed on my local computer, so let's run a command against this subscription. I'll just run the az group list command.

Now let's look at the menu across the top. If you have problems starting the Cloud Shell, like if it hangs during connection, you can restart it from here. This can come in handy. You can upload and download files. You might have scripts you want to run here or you might upload a file with variables that you want to use when running commands. Remember, there is a file share attached, so those files are only accessible to you. You can actually see the files and edit them right here too. If I expand this and click on a file, it opens in the editor on the right, and I can modify the contents, but let's hide this and now let's switch over to the PowerShell version of the Cloud Shell.

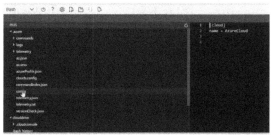

I'll just confirm, and the terminal connects again. I'm already authenticated in the portal, so I can run PowerShell commands here.

Before we leave the Cloud Shell, I just want to show you that besides accessing it here in the Azure portal, you can also go to shell.azure.com, and that opens a full screen version of the Azure Cloud Shell. Depending on your device format, that might be easier to use.

Chapter 55 Azure Resource Manager Templates

Now let's talk about using Azure Resource Manager templates to deploy resources in a repeatable way. Many development teams are adopting agile methods and quick iterations where they want to deploy repeatedly and know that their infrastructure is in a reliable state. That's a big part of DevOps where the traditional division between developers and IT operations roles has disappeared. Teams are now managing infrastructure using code, so those definitions can be stored in code repositories alongside the source code, and they can be deployed in repeatable ways, sometimes using the same continuous integration continuous deployment process that's used to deploy web applications and database code. To implement infrastructure as code, Azure has Resource Manager templates. These are files written using JavaScript Object Notation, or JSON, and the contents define the infrastructure and configuration for all the Azure resources in your solution. It uses a declarative syntax, which means you state what you intend to deploy without having to write a series of programming commands to create it. Once you write the code in the template, you can deploy it in a variety of ways. In the Azure DevOps service, Azure Pipelines allow you to automate code deployments to hosting environments and you can deploy Resource Manager templates as part of an Azure Pipeline too. You can also deploy templates from within GitHub using GitHub Actions, which is a service that's similar to Azure Pipelines. It's also possible to deploy templates using PowerShell or the Azure CLI, and you can also deploy templates using the Azure portal. Let's take a look at how to do that. I'll open up the list of resource groups and drill into the one we created using the Azure CLI. There are three resources in this resource group, an app service, an app service plan, and a storage account.

Every resource in Azure is defined by an ARM template. Let's look at this storage account. If we go down to the export template tab at the bottom, Azure will generate an ARM template based on the current configuration.

Parameters are broken out by default, so it's easy to change the name of the storage account when you deploy a new one using this template, but you can turn off that feature and have the name generated inline in the JSON.

Often, you'll want to deploy groups of resources though, so let's go back to the resource group and there is a tab on the menu here too that will generate an ARM template with all the resources in this resource group, but it's also possible to select just the resources you want and export the template from the menu here at the top. Now we've got just the app service plan, which is called serverFarms in the JSON, and the app service whose resource type is actually called microsoft.web/sites. From this screen, you can download the template and that creates a zip file with the template and a file with the parameters.

Export resource group template

↓ Download ⊟ Add to library ⫶ Deploy ⫶⫶ Visualize template

ⓘ To export related resources, select the resources from the Resource Group view then select the "Export template" option from the tool bar.

☑ Include parameters ⓘ

Template   Parameters   Scripts

```
                                    1  {
> ⟨⟩ Parameters (2)                  2    "$schema": "https://schema.management.azure.com/schemas/2019-04-01/deploymentTemplate.json#",
  ⟨⟩ Variables (0)                   3    "contentVersion": "1.0.0.0",
∨ ⟨⟩ Resources (8)                   4    "parameters": {
   ■ [parameters('serverfarms_asp_from 5      "sites_webinmfromcli_name": {
     (Microsoft.Web/serverfarms)      6        "defaultValue": "webinmfromcli",
   ⊗ [parameters('sites_webinmfromcli 7        "type": "String"
     (Microsoft.Web/sites)            8      },
     [concat(parameters('sites_webinm 9      "serverfarms_asp_fromcli_name": {
   ⟨⟩ '/ftp')]                       10        "defaultValue": "asp-fromcli",
     (Microsoft.Web/sites/basicPublish 11       "type": "String"
     [concat(parameters('sites_webinm 12      }
   ⟨⟩ /scm')]                        13    },
     (Microsoft.Web/sites/basicPublish 14    "variables": {},
     [concat(parameters('sites_webinm 15    "resources": [
   ⟨⟩ /web')]                        16      {
     (Microsoft.Web/sites/config)     17        "type": "Microsoft.Web/serverfarms",
     [concat(parameters('sites_webinm 18        "apiVersion": "2022-03-01",
   ⟨⟩ '/'                            19        "name": "[parameters('serverfarms_asp_fromcli_name')]",
   ∨ parameters('sites_webinmfromcli 20        "location": "Canada Central",
     azurewebsites.net')]            21        "sku": {
     (Microsoft.Web/sites/hostNameBi 22          "name": "S1",
     [concat(parameters('sites_webinm 23          "tier": "Standard",
   ⟨⟩ '/2022-08-                     24          "size": "S1",
     31T16_17_57_2723609')]          25          "family": "S",
     (Microsoft.Web/sites/snapshots)  26          "capacity": 1
     [concat(parameters('sites_webinm 27        },
   ⟨⟩ '/2022-08-                     28        "kind": "app",
     31T16_17_57_3104302')]          29        "properties": {
     (Microsoft.Web/sites/snapshots)  30          "perSiteScaling": false,
                                     31          "elasticScaleEnabled": false,
                                     32          "maximumElasticWorkerCount": 1,
                                     33          "isSpot": false,
```

If I double-click the template file, it opens in Visual Studio Code, which is the default editor on my local computer. So you could use this as a starting place and modify it to configure or add resources.

```
template.json  ×

C: > Users > mahn > AppData > Local > Temp > Temp1.ExportedTemplate-ck-hp.np > {} template.json >
 1   {
 2       "$schema": "https://schema.management.azure.com/schemas/2019-04-01/deploymentTemplate.json#",
 3       "contentVersion": "1.0.0.0",
 4       "parameters": {
 5           "sites_webinmfromcli_name": {
 6               "defaultValue": "webinmfromcli",
 7               "type": "String"
 8           },
 9           "serverfarms_asp_fromcli_name": {
10               "defaultValue": "asp-fromcli",
11               "type": "String"
12           }
13       },
14       "variables": {},
15       "resources": [
16           {
17               "type": "Microsoft.Web/serverfarms",
18               "apiVersion": "2022-03-01",
19               "name": "[parameters('serverfarms_asp_fromcli_name')]",
20               "location": "Canada Central",
21               "sku": {
22                   "name": "S1",
23                   "tier": "Standard",
24                   "size": "S1",
25                   "family": "S",
26                   "capacity": 1
27               },
28               "kind": "app",
29               "properties": {
30                   "perSiteScaling": false,
31                   "elasticScaleEnabled": false,
32                   "maximumElasticWorkerCount": 1,
33                   "isSpot": false,
34                   "reserved": false,
35                   "isXenon": false,
36                   "hyperV": false,
37                   "targetWorkerCount": 0,
38                   "targetWorkerSizeId": 0,
39                   "zoneRedundant": false
40               }
```

Let's go back to the browser though and let's see how we can deploy the template from here. Now when you're generating a template like this from the existing state of deployed resources, you often need to massage it a bit.

Besides changing the names of resources to deploy new instances, sometimes there are things included that actually can't get deployed. Let's edit this template. I'll scroll down to the bottom, and there are two entries for snapshots.

```
            }
    {
        "type": "Microsoft.Web/sites/snapshots",
        "apiVersion": "2015-08-01",
        "name": "[concat(parameters('sites_webinmfromcli_name'), '/2022-08-31T18_37_57_2733609')]",
        "dependsOn": [
            "[resourceId('Microsoft.Web/sites', parameters('sites_webinmfromcli_name'))]"
        ]
    },
    {
        "type": "Microsoft.Web/sites/snapshots",
        "apiVersion": "2015-08-01",
        "name": "[concat(parameters('sites_webinmfromcli_name'), '/2022-08-31T19_37_57_3104202')]",
        "dependsOn": [
            "[resourceId('Microsoft.Web/sites', parameters('sites_webinmfromcli_name'))]"
        ]
    }
]
```

The documentation says that these are read-only, which means they can't be deployed, so let's remove them and let's save these changes. Okay, now let's create a new resource group to deploy this template to. The parameters from the template are showing here, so let's change the name of the app service and the app service plan.

That's all we need to do. The validation passed, so let's create this.

Custom deployment
Deploy from a custom template

✓ Validation Passed

Basics   Review + create

Summary

Customized template
6 resources

It'll take about a minute to deploy the resources in the template.

And it says the deployment is complete. Let's go to the Resource groups tab and there is the new resource group. There is an app service and an app service plan. Let's drill into the app service, and I'll just click browse to make sure it's running.

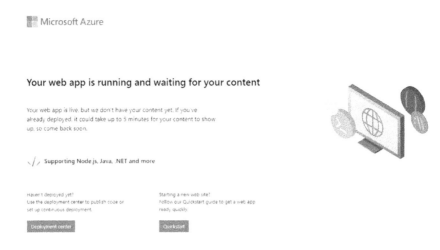

So that's how you can use Azure Resource Manager templates to deploy resources in a repeatable way. Next, let's talk about monitoring the health of the Azure platform.

Chapter 56 Azure Service Health

Azure Service Health keeps you informed about the health of your cloud resources. This includes information about current and upcoming issues that might impact your deployed resources like outages and planned maintenance. There is actually three services that make up service health. Azure status gives you information on service outages across all of Azure, Service Health is a personalized view of the services and regions that you're actually using, and Resource health provides information on your specific resources. Let's look at these. Azure status isn't part of the Azure portal. You go to azure.status.microsoft. It gives you an overview of all the Azure services and their current status. So this is a high-level view of Azure.

The regions are organized into high-level groupings with each region and columns and Azure services and rows, it's quite a long list of services. Let's go to the Azure portal and look at Service Health, which is the recommended way to check the health of your resources. I'll search for it under All services.

So Service Health scopes the affected services to just the ones that you use, so you might not be impacted by an outage in Azure Front Door, for example, if you're not using that service. Azure Service Health will trim those notifications to just what matters to you. You can find out about planned maintenance in Azure that might affect you, so you might want to notify clients of an upcoming event or reschedule an application deployment. There is some planned maintenance here for Azure App Service in regions where I have app services deployed. Notice the impact category says that there is no impact expected.

Health advisories are changes in Azure services that require your attention. For example, if features in a service that you use are being deprecated or you need to upgrade your web applications because the framework version in Azure App Service is being updated.

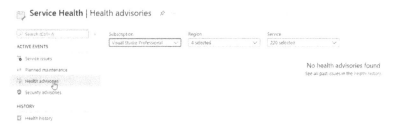

There is also a link to Health history here which has one of the same links from planned maintenance, but also this historical entry about a DNS failure with Azure Monitor. Security Advisories are notifications or violations that might affect the availability of your Azure services.

The Resource health tab lets you scope to just certain resource types in your subscriptions.

The first two app services are grayed out because they're on a free pricing tier where resource health isn't available, but these other two are on the standard pricing tier, so you can get a quick summary of the overall health and drill in to see more.

If there were issues here, there would also be information on actions that Microsoft is taking to fix the problems and it would identify things that you can do to address them.

You can see a history of the health of the resource if you need to do some historical troubleshooting, and you can add a health alert from here also. Let's back out and let's add a service health alert. You can use this to be notified when there are any changes to a particular service, you can filter the alerts to just service issues or health advisories, security alerts, or planned maintenance, and you can filter the services and regions that you want to be notified about.

The alerts get sent to an action group. Let's open this up and create a new action group. Let's just move ahead to the Notifications tab.

You can just have an email sent to the people in the Resource Manager role, or you can set up a custom notification for email, text message, and automated voice message, and there is an option here for Azure app push notifications.

You can get notified on your mobile device through the Azure app too. So Azure Service Health can make you aware of when there is an issue with the underlying platform that can prevent you from chasing down a problem with your application when it isn't your application at all. But sometimes the problem isn't with the entire service, it's with your resource. So let's look at how to monitor resources next.

Chapter 57 How to use Azure Monitor

Azure Monitor is a service in Azure that collects metrics and logs from the Azure resources in your subscription. You can use these to check on the performance and availability of your applications and services. Metrics are numerical values that describe some aspect of a system at a particular point in time, and they're constantly being collected. This could be things like the response time of a web application, the amount of CPU being used on a VM, the amount of data coming out of a storage account. Metrics are good for alerting and fast detection of issues. The tool in Azure Monitor that helps you explore the collected metrics is called Metrics Explorer, and it's available inside each Azure resource. Logs, on the other hand, are different kinds of data that are organized into records with different properties for each type of log entry. Logs are good for troubleshooting issues and for analyzing trends. Azure Monitor includes a tool called Log Analytics, which is used to edit and run queries on the log data. It uses a powerful query language called the Kusto Query Language that's kind of like SQL, and it lets you sort, filter, and visualize the data in charts. Another service that's part of Azure Monitor is Application Insights. This monitors the availability, performance, and usage of your web applications. For Azure App Service, you can turn on Application Insights and it will monitor your app from the hosting environment, so things like performance counters on the servers, Docker logs, and you can set up web tests to send requests to your application. You can track API calls and dependencies outside of your application also. For deeper monitoring, you can use the Application Insights SDK to include instrumentation right in your code, and it's available for a number of programming languages. So your application doesn't need to be hosted in Azure to send data to Application Insights from the SDK. Let's take a look at the documentation.

Metrics and logs are collected from different sources inside Azure, and you can collect data from virtual machines outside Azure by installing agents on the machines. Then the data is stored as metrics, logs, and traces, and traces refers to distributed traces. When you have an application with different components deployed to different virtual machines or app services or containers, distributed traces are the data gathered from each of those hosts so it traces a web request through the different tiers of the application and all that data is linked together through some correlation id, which is all possible by using Application Insights. The data that gets collected by Azure Monitor gets used in different ways. Experiences are visualizations and queries that are organized for you already. You'll see shortly in Azure Monitor that these are also called Insights with Application Insights being one of them. You can visualize the data in Azure Monitor using dashboards and a Microsoft service called Power BI. There are tools in the Azure portal to inspect the metrics and log analytics for querying the logs, and you can respond to changes in the metrics by setting up alerts and performing actions like autoscaling an app service to add virtual machines when the load is heavy or calling other services to perform an action like a Logic app.

Chapter 58 How to Explore Azure Monitor

Now let's take a look at Azure Monitor in the Azure portal. Let's look at the central Azure monitor service in this subscription.

On the overview page, there are shortcuts to the same things as on the menu on the left. Metrics are all the metrics collected by the different resources we've deployed. You need to drill into individual resources in order to view the metrics. If I apply this, the metrics are scoped to the ones that are relevant just to this app service, like average response time and the number of requests. Logs are where you can query the logs sent to your Log Analytics workspace.

There are pre-built queries here to get you started and they fall into categories like alerts, audit logs for Azure Active Directory. You can actually send metrics to Log Analytics too so they can be queried like other logs. And there are performance queries here related to Azure functions. Let's just pick a query and run it. This shows you the syntax of the Kusto Query Language so you can start to write your own queries.

You can access Service Health from within Azure Monitor too. Insights are referred to as curated visualizations. It's a customized monitoring experience for a particular service. Application Insights is for web applications, and it can collect information from outside the application from the hosting platform, as well as from inside the code of your web application.

The virtual machine insights allows you to monitor the health and performance of your windows and Linux VMs inside Azure, as well as virtual machines hosted on-premises or even in other cloud environments. To enable that, you need to install an agent on the virtual machines to send data to Azure Monitor. You can monitor the overall health of your storage accounts. There are some metrics here, and the Capacity tab tells you the amount of storage being used by each service in the storage account. Network insights gives you a view of the health and metrics for all your deployed networking resources.

This is good for checking on application gateways and load balancers, but not all networking resources have health checks. You can also set up connectivity tests to monitor things like latency between VMs and storage and applications hosted in Azure and on-premises, which also requires installing agents to run the connectivity tests. Let's take a look at setting up alerts for metrics in Azure Monitor. Up at the top of the menu is the Alerts tab. From here, you can create an alert rule. Let's create an alert for an app service.

Next, we set up conditions for the alert. There is a number of metrics to choose from here. Let's select CPU time.

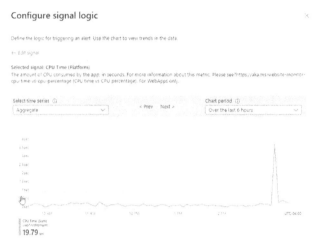

Define the logic for triggering an alert. Use the chart to view trends in the data.

← Edit signal

Selected signal: CPU Time (Platform)
The amount of CPU consumed by the app, in seconds. For more information about this metric. Please see https://aka.ms/website-monitor-cpu-time-vs-cpu-percentage (CPU time vs CPU percentage). For WebApps only.

Select time series ⓘ			Chart period ⓘ	
Aggregate	⌄	< Prev Next >	Over the last 6 hours	⌄

CPU Time (Sum)
web1confrgmgmt
19.79

This is the amount of CPU consumed by the app in seconds. We could scope this metric to a particular virtual machine in the underlying app service plan if there is more than one. And we can set the alert logic so when the total CPU time is greater than 80 seconds, then the alert will get fired. Let's finish this part. And next, you decide what happens when the alert is fired. Just like with the service health alerts, you do that with an action group. We don't have any created, so let's create one.

Create an action group

Basics   Notifications   Actions   Tags   Review + create

An action group invokes a defined set of notifications and actions when an alert is triggered. Learn more

Project details

Select a subscription to manage deployed resources and costs. Use resource groups like folders to organize and manage all your resources.

Subscription * ⓘ	Visual Studio Professional	⌄
Resource group * ⓘ		⌄
	Select existing	
Region *	arm_rg	⌄
Instance details	dk_rg	
Action group name * ⓘ	cloud-shell-storage-eastus	
	DefaultResourceGroup-EYA	

I'll create it in the same resource group and give this action group a name. And next, we set up the notification type. I'll choose the push notification option, and this can be an email, text message, voice message, or we can push out a notification to the Azure app on the mobile device of this user. Let's give this notification a name.

And besides sending a notification, you can also configure an action when the alert is fired. That could be calling an Azure function or a Logic app, calling a webhook in an outside web service.

There is lots of options for taking actions when an alert gets fired. We'll skip tags and let's create this action group. And now let's create the alert rule. Now let's move forward and create this alert.

You can see all the alerts from the Alert Rules tab at the top. Next, let's look at using Azure Monitor metrics and logs from right inside Azure resources.

Chapter 59 How to Use Azure Monitor Metrics in a Resource

Azure Monitor collects metrics for Azure services by default, it's turned on automatically. So let's navigate into a service that we've created like this app service we deployed earlier using an ARM template.

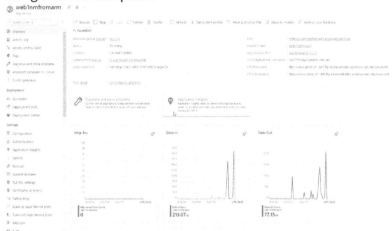

Right on the overview page, there are charts showing things like HTTP server errors, the amount of data moving in and out of the app service, the number of requests, and the average response time. These are coming from Azure Monitor and these are just predefined views of the metrics that are being collected. You can dig deeper by going down the menu to the Monitoring group and clicking Metrics.

Most Azure resources have a Monitoring section on the menu, although the exact tabs might be different depending on the service. We have a blank slate here. Because we're inside a resource already, some of these items are already populated like the scope of the resource and the metric namespace. The same metrics are here that you saw on the charts on the overview page, but there are others too like CPU time for the underlying virtual machines in the app service plan. Let's select that. It shows a slight spike here around 6 PM.

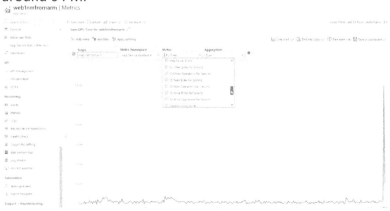

If we scroll further down the list, there are all sorts of metrics around IO, and there is the number of requests. Let's choose that.

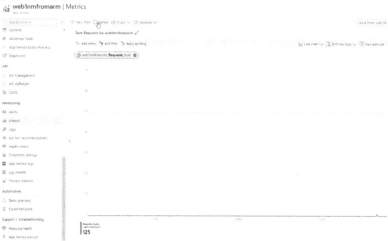

It shows 125 total requests. With these charts, you can choose a different aggregation. So instead of summing all the requests, we could show the count at different time periods or the average requests. Let's try a different metric like Private Bytes, which is the working memory set on the server that the app service has allocated.

If this number keeps growing, you might have a memory leak in your application. Depending on the resource, you can apply splitting to the graph. In the case of an app service, I've increased the instance count of the underlying app service plan, so there are two virtual machines, and we can split the graph to show how the metric, Private Bytes in this case, applies to each VM. Let's see what that looks like for a different metric. Let's try Response Time.

It looks like there is quite a difference here, but that's probably because I just added the second instance a short time ago, so it hasn't serviced many requests. Across the top, you can give the chart a name, and you can pin it to the dashboard so it will show up on the main dashboard page along with any other charts and graphs that you want to see every time you log in. That's a quick look at metrics in this app service. Let's look at logs next.

Chapter 60 Log Analytics in Azure Monitor

Now let's look at Logs. I'm still inside the app service. There are a bunch of predefined queries that you can run against the log data that's been collected, but before we can do that, we have to enable that log collection.

You do that from the Diagnostic settings. Let's add a diagnostic setting. Depending on the resource you're in, there are different types of logs available, and you can choose to send metrics also.

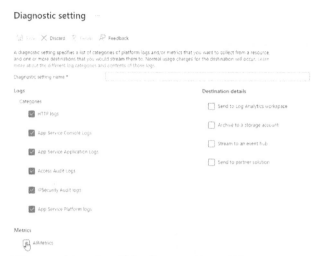

We need to give this diagnostic setting a name and then you choose where you want to send the logs. Log Analytics is the obvious choice where you can aggregate all your logs together and run queries. There is a default workspace created automatically, but you can have multiple Log Analytics workspaces. You can send these logs to a storage account and specify how long you want to retain each of the log types for. You can stream the logs to an event hub where they can get ingested by another Azure service or you can send the logs to a third-party tool, maybe you have one in your organization already and you want to keep all the logs together. Let's just send these logs to Log Analytics and save this setting. Now that we have a diagnostic setting, we can go to the Logs tab, which lets us run queries against the data. You can choose a pre-built query from here, and these queries fall into the categories on the left menu.

Let's scroll down and choose the query related to response times. This is actually a metric that's being sent to Log Analytics. You can see the Kusto Query Language syntax here, and this is a good way to learn how to write queries by using these pre-built ones.

We just turned on logging so there won't be any data yet. I'll go to the default page in the app service, which is already open, and keep refreshing it so there is data generated. It won't show up right away in the logs, but it will come back later when the data is available. There is a chart generated from the results of this query, and the individual data is showing on the Results tab.

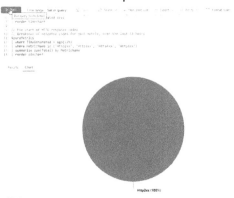

So even though this is metric data like we saw in the metrics demo, because it was sent to Log Analytics, there is individual records for each web response here, it's not aggregated like in the Metrics Explorer. Let's try a different query, the one for HTTP response codes. It's showing that all the response codes were in the 200s, which indicates successful HTTP responses.

You can do some formatting of the chart from right here, and across the top, you have some options. You can share this query, you can create an alert based on this query, and you can export the query results to a CSV file, Excel, or to Power BI, and you can also pin the query to the dashboard just like on the Metrics tab. Let's navigate out of here and look at another resource group. This one has a storage account. Let's open that up. And down the menu on the storage account, there is a Monitoring section here too.

Some of the items are different from the app service, but we've got logs and metrics here too. You can scope the metrics to each of the services in the storage account and there are different metrics here that apply to Azure storage, so things like the count of blobs in the containers or the ingress of the data that I uploaded.

On the Logs tab, there are custom queries here related to storage, and you still need to turn on logging from the Diagnostic settings, but here you can set up logging on the individual services in the storage account. That's a quick look at logs. Remember, in the central Azure Monitor service, you can access the logs for all the resources you've configured to send logs to Azure Monitor, then you can write custom queries to correlate data across services. Next, let's look at Azure Advisor.

Chapter 61 How to Optimize Resources using Azure Advisor

Microsoft refers to Azure Advisor as a personalized cloud consultant that helps you follow best practices to optimize your Azure deployments. It's actually a great tool to provide recommendations on how to improve performance, availability, and security of your Azure resources, as well as recommending ways that you can save on costs in Azure. Let's go to All services and search for advisor, and click on here to open up Azure Advisor. It refreshes your recommendations when it loads.

These are personalized recommendations, so Azure is looking at the resources that you have deployed, it's not just providing a list of generic recommendations. This dashboard provides a summary of the recommendations broken down by five categories, cost, security, reliability, operational excellence, and performance. You can click on the tiles at the bottom to get links to each of the recommendations or you can use the menu on the left. Let's look at the security recommendations.

The first one says Accounts with owner permissions should be MFA enabled. So it's telling me to enable multifactor authentication on all the administrator accounts. There is a medium impact recommendation that storage accounts should use a private link connection. Some of these might not make sense for the design of your solution, so you can actually turn these off individually so you don't keep seeing them. Let's go to the next page. Here is one that has a quick fix.

It says web application should only be accessible over HTTPS. Let's click this. On the remediation steps, it says I can just select the app service and click the Fix button.

Web Application should only be accessible over HTTPS

It will turn on a setting in the app service that only allows incoming traffic over HTTPS so HTTP is disabled. So in some cases, Azure Advisor can make the required changes for you, otherwise, it will just describe what you need to do. Let's go back to the main screen and let's look at the Reliability tab.

There is just one recommendation and it's for the virtual network being used by the virtual machine that I created. It says add NAT gateway to your subnets to go outbound. If I click on the link, it brings me to a screen to create a NAT gateway.

Create network address translation (NAT) gateway

Basics   Outbound IP   Subnet   Tags   Review + create

Azure NAT gateway can be used to translate outbound flows from a virtual network to the public internet.
Learn more about NAT gateways.

Project details

Select a subscription to manage deployed resources and costs. Use resource groups like folders to organize and manage all
your resources.

Subscription *   Visual Studio Professional

    Resource group *
                      Create new

Instance details

NAT gateway name *

Region *   East US

Availability zone   None

TCP idle timeout (minutes) *   4
                                                        4-120

In this case, it isn't fixing the problem for me, but it's making it easier to fix. We won't complete this though. Let's go back and move on to cost recommendations. There actually aren't any, but there is this link to the list of cost recommendations that Azure Advisor uses.

This is a way to be proactive and configure your resources to best save on costs. The first recommendation is for compute and it says to use standard storage for disk snapshots rather than using premium storage. For another service like Azure storage, it has a recommendation about retention policies for log data so you're not storing old data you'll never use. Operational excellence has to do with deployment best practices and things like creating service health alerts. I don't have any recommendations here and performances to help improve the speed of the applications I have deployed. Again, you can view the standard list of recommendations here to get an idea of what Azure Advisor looks for. The last thing I want to show you is on the Overview page.

At the bottom, you can download the recommendations in PDF and CSV format, so you could share this report with other team members who might not have access to the Azure portal. Next, let's step outside of the Azure portal and look at the Azure app, which allows managing Azure from your mobile device.

Chapter 62 Azure App for Mobile Devices

Let's take a look at the Azure app. This is a tool that lets you monitor the health and status of your Azure resources, quickly diagnose and fix issues, and you can even run commands using the Cloud Shell.

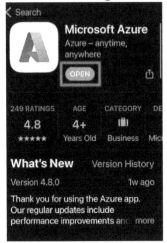

You can download the app from the Apple App Store and from Google Play. I've already installed the app on my iPhone so let's open it up. I'm logged in and I've chosen a subscription. On the home page here, any alerts would show right away. I don't have any so let's scroll down, and I have access to Service Health from here too.

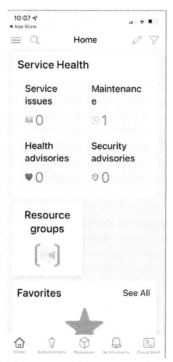

Service Health

Service issues

0

Maintenance

1

Health advisories

0

Security advisories

0

Resource groups

Favorites   See All

Home   Subscriptions   Resources   Notifications   Cloud Shell

There aren't any service issues, but there is a maintenance notification. It's something about routine maintenance on app services. So I can see the Maintenance window and the impacted regions, and there is more detail further down. It says there is no impact expected.

2022-08-23 1:12:03 AM

Service: App Service
Region(s): Australia Central,
Australia East, South Africa North,
West US 3, East Asia, Canada
Central, UK West, East US 2,
West US, Korea South, South
Central US
Stage: Planned
Impact Category: No impact
expected
You're receiving this
notification because you
currently use App Service.
Summary: Azure App Service will
begin upgrading your resources
as part of routine scheduled
maintenance in around 7 days.
Once started in a given region,
upgrades generally take between
24-78 hours to complete. You
may receive more than one
notification per region if a
subscription has resources on

Back on the home screen, you can create shortcuts to resources that you frequently check on. Let's open up all the resource groups. I'm going to open up a resource group where I know there is a storage account. There is cost management information here showing how much this resource group is costing me.

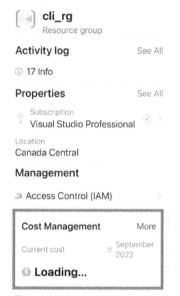

cli_rg
Resource group

Activity log　　　　See All

ⓘ 17 Info

Properties　　　　See All

Subscription
Visual Studio Professional ⊘ ›

Location
Canada Central

Management

▵ Access Control (IAM)　　　›

Cost Management　　　More

Current cost　　　September 2022

🌐 **Loading...**

Resources

At the bottom are the resources, so I'll drill into this storage account. I can see some metrics that show me the health of the storage account, and these are coming from Azure Monitor. The Resource health tells me that the storage account is available.

Activity log　　　　See All

ⓘ 1 Info

Metrics　　　　See All

Average success E2E latency

‐‐ Success E2E Latency

• • • •

Resource health

⊘ Available　　　›

Properties　　　　See All

Subscription
Visual Studio Professional ⊘ ›

There is some information about the resource, and at the bottom is Access Control. So I can give someone access to the storage account from here, which can be handy if you're out of the office and there is an issue or a new client needs to upload files.

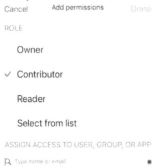

Let's back out of here and go back to the list of resource groups. I'll choose one that has a virtual machine in it. I'll open up this virtual machine. You can see the metrics for the virtual machine and you can restart the VM from here if there is a problem.

I'll actually shut it down so I don't incur compute charges. And you can even connect to this VM. This button will launch another app, Microsoft Remote Desktop. Let's back out of here and go back to the home screen. At the bottom, you can open up the Cloud Shell.

You can choose between the Bash Shell and PowerShell, and from here, you can type in PowerShell and Azure CLI commands to manage your resources. Let's run this az group list command, and we get back information on all the resource groups in the subscription.

```
{
    "id": "/subscriptions/0ef1dba3-743c
-4fe2-97bf-8d81c3e64c20/resourceGroups/
websitesRG",
    "location": "centralus",
    "managedBy": null,
    "name": "websitesRG",
    "properties": {
        "provisioningState": "Succeeded"
    },
    "tags": null,
    "type": "Microsoft.Resources/resour
ceGroups"
},
{
    "id": "/subscriptions/0ef1dba3-743c
-4fe2-97bf-8d81c3e64c20/resourceGroups/
pieshoprg",
    "location": "canadacentral",
    "managedBy": null,
    "name": "pieshoprg",
    "properties": {
        "provisioningState": "Succeeded"
    },
    "tags": null,
    "type": "Microsoft.Resources/resour
ceGroups"
},
{
    "id": "/subscriptions/0ef1dba3-743c
-4fe2-97bf-8d81c3e64c20/resourceGroups/
pssamples",
    "location": "eastus2",
    "managedBy": null,
    "name": "pssamples",
    "properties": {
```

We can switch to PowerShell and it will restart the Cloud Shell. The last thing I want to show you is that from the menu at the top left, you can manage your log in and change directories, and you can even access support requests from here.

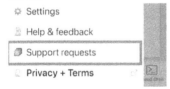

So the Azure app provides an easy way to perform some Azure management tasks from your mobile device. Next, let's talk about Azure Arc.

Chapter 63 How to Manage Resources Outside Azure using Azure Arc

Azure Arc is a service in Azure that allows you to manage resources outside of Azure. So resources that you host on-premises or in other cloud platforms like Amazon Web Services or Google Cloud. You can manage a few different types of resources hosted outside of Azure. You can manage Windows and Linux physical servers and virtual machines, that means being able to monitor them, secure them, and update them from within Azure Arc. When you're hosting your virtual machines on private cloud platforms like VMware vSphere or Azure Stack HCI, you get additional integration with Azure Arc like the ability to perform lifecycle operations like provisioning, restarting, resizing, and deleting virtual machines as if they were hosted in Azure. SQL Server instances hosted outside of Azure can be managed using Azure Arc also, and with Azure Arc, you can manage Kubernetes clusters running on-premises and with other cloud providers. Remember, Kubernetes is an orchestration service for containers. You can apply Azure policies to the Kubernetes clusters to enforce configuration and compliance. Once you have Kubernetes clusters being managed, you can run other Azure services on them like data services. SQL managed instances and postgreSQL hyperscale databases are available running on Kubernetes. You can deploy Azure machine learning workloads onto those clusters also. And you can deploy Azure App Services on Azure Arc-enabled Kubernetes clusters, including web apps, function apps, and even Logic apps so your developers can leverage the features of app service while you maintain corporate compliance by hosting the app services on internal infrastructure or leveraging your existing investment with other cloud providers. You get features of Azure Resource Manager when your resources are managed using Azure Arc. That includes organizing resources using management groups and tags, searching and indexing them using Azure Resource Graph, security and access control through role-based access control and subscriptions, automation using templates and extensions, and update management. For physical and virtual machines hosted outside Azure that you want to manage with Azure Arc, you install the Azure connected machine agent on the servers. That lets you proactively monitor the operating system and workloads running on the machine, and you can leverage Azure features like update management to manage operating system updates. You can apply Azure policies to audit settings inside the machine. You can leverage Microsoft Defender for threat detection and Microsoft Sentinel to collect security-related events, and you can collect log data using the Log Analytics agent. The data gets sent to a Log Analytics workspace.

Chapter 64 How to Add Local Server to Azure Arc

Let's look at Azure Arc in the Azure portal. I'll go to All services and search for Arc. When Azure Arc opens, all the infrastructure services that can be hosted are listed on the menu.

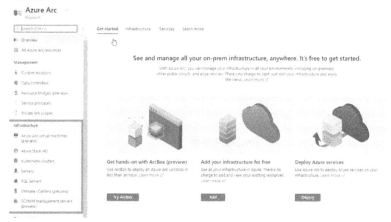

The data services are below and the application services are below that. Let's go to Servers. These are the physical and virtual servers that you host on-premises or in cloud environments other than Azure. There aren't any being hosted, so let's add one. I'll add a single server, and this will be a virtual machine running on my local computer using Hyper-V.

It says the server will need HTTPS access to Azure services for outbound connectivity. It'll need local admin permissions and the server can connect over a public endpoint, so over the internet, or using a private endpoint. We also need an existing resource group to add the server to. I'll click Next, and I've already created a resource group for this which will change the region to Canada Central.

This VM will be using the Windows operating system, but it could use Linux. And connectivity will be over the internet. Next, we can fill out some tags. The default ones define the location of the server. You can add your own custom ones also. On the next page, a script is generated. We need to run this script on the local server in order to download and install the agent and connect the server to Azure Arc, so I'll copy this script. And I have this virtual machine running on my local computer using Hyper-V. I'll search for PowerShell and open it up as an administrator. Now I'll paste in the script I copied from the Azure portal, and let's run this script on the local VM. It'll take a few minutes because it's downloading the agent from Azure.

```
    Invoke-WebRequest -Uri "https://gb1.his.arc.azure.com/log" -Method "PUT" -Body ($logBody | ConvertTo-
    Write-Host  -ForegroundColor red $_.Exception
}

VERBOSE: Installing Azure Connected Machine Agent
VERBOSE: .NET Framework version: 4.7.3190
VERBOSE: Downloading agent package
VERBOSE: Installing agent package
Installation of azcmagent completed successfully
time="2022-09-05T13:43:57-04:00" level=info msg="Connecting Machine. This might take a few minutes."
To sign in, use a web browser to open the page https://microsoft.com/devicelogin and enter the code E
Q6DB2Y62 to authenticate.
```

Next it's asking me to sign into Azure by going to
microsoft.com/devicelogin and entering the code here. So
let's open up a browser and navigate to the URL and it's
asking for the code, so I'll switch back to PowerShell to enter
it in. Now I need to authenticate. My administrator account
has already logged into the browser so I'll use that and it has
MFA enabled, so I get a code sent to my phone. I'll enter that
in, and now it says Are you trying to sign in to Azure
Connected Machine Agent?

So I'll hit Continue, and now we can go back to PowerShell,
and   it'll   continue   with   the   installation.

```
  50% [[32m=[0m[32m=[0m[32m=[0m[32m=[0m[32m=[0m[32m=[0m[32m=[0m[32m>[0m          ] [0m

  80% [[32m=[0m[32m=[0m[32m=[0m[32m=[0m[32m=[0m[32m=[0m[32m=[0m[32m=[0m[32m=[0m[32m=[0m[32m=[0m[32m=[0m[32
m=[0m[32m=[0m[32m>[0m      ] [0m

 100% [[32m=[0m[32m=[0m[32m=[0m[32m=[0m[32m=[0m[32m=[0m[32m=[0m[32m=[0m[32m=[0m[32m=[0m[32m=[0m[32
m=[0m[32m=[0m[32m=[0m[32m=[0m[32m=[0m[32m=[0m[32m=[0m[32m=[0m]  [0mtime="2022-09-05T13:46:24-04:00" level
=info msg="Successfully connected machine to Azure\n"
time="2022-09-05T13:46:24-04:00" level=info msg="Machine overview page: https://portal.azure.com/#@3d
2faa73-87ca-4f25-adb8-71214334f8d5/resource/subscriptions/0ef1dba3-743c-4fe2-97bf-8d81c3e64c20/resour
ceGroups/arc_rg/providers/Microsoft.HybridCompute/machines/WIN-CJ9M8IT3BCT/overview"

PS C:\Users\Administrator> |
```

Once that's done, the machine should be getting managed
by Azure Arc. Let's go back to the Azure portal. I'll close out
of this and out of the Add server screen, and we're already
on the Servers tab so I'll just hit Refresh. There is the server
that was added and it says it's connected. There is

information here about the operating system and tabs along the left with actions we can perform on this VM. Let's look at Security. Microsoft Defender is running on this virtual machine now, so it's scanning for threats, and there are also recommendations being made related to security.

One of them says that Log Analytics agent should be installed on Windows-based Azure Arc-enabled machines. So Log Analytics doesn't get installed by default, that's another agent we can install on the local VM. We can also manage operating system updates on this VM using Azure automation, and there is something called Automanage that will apply a preset configuration to the VM depending on whether it's being used for dev or production, and that includes things like backup and monitoring.

You can also assign policies to the VM so you can assess it for compliance to rules set up in Azure Policy. There is a lot of functionality here that makes it seem like this virtual machine is running right inside Azure, but of course, it's not, it's running on my local computer. So Azure Arc provides a lot of possibilities for simplifying your resource management across other clouds and on-premises. Let's have a quick review of what you've learned. We started with understanding how Azure is implemented physically with regions and data centers and logically with subscriptions and resource groups. You saw how to use the Azure portal and learned a bit about Azure Active Directory for controlling access. Next you learned about Azure compute. We looked at virtual machines, containers, and Azure App Services for hosting web apps, as well as Azure Functions for smaller pieces of code. Then you saw some of the main features of networking in Azure, like virtual networks, network security groups, Azure DNS, and private endpoints. You also learned about connecting your on-premises network to Azure using VPN Gateway and ExpressRoute. Then you learned about data storage in Azure with Azure Storage accounts, including how to copy files in Azure and migrate data into the cloud. Then you learned about managing and monitoring Azure using features like the Azure CLI and Resource Manager templates and services like Azure Monitor and Azure Arc. We've covered a lot in Azure, but there are a lot more features and services that are worth checking out like solutions for big data ingestion and analysis, solutions for the Internet of Things, machine learning services, and artificial intelligence. Those things actually used to be part of the AZ-900 Azure Fundamentals exam, but they were removed probably because they're pretty advanced and aren't relevant to as many people as these topics, but I encourage you to jump in and try Azure, create a free trial account, and take some of the services for a drive.

Conclusion

Congratulations on completing this book! I am sure you have plenty on your belt, but please don't forget to leave an honest review. Furthermore, if you think this information was helpful to you, please share anyone who you think would be interested of IT as well.

About Richie Miller

Richie Miller has always loved teaching people Technology. He graduated with a degree in radio production with a minor in theatre in order to be a better communicator. While teaching at the Miami Radio and Television Broadcasting Academy, Richie was able to do voiceover work at a technical training company specializing in live online classes in Microsoft, Cisco, and CompTia technologies. Over the years, he became one of the top virtual instructors at several training companies, while also speaking at many tech and training conferences. Richie specializes in Project Management and ITIL these days, while also doing his best to be a good husband and father.

www.ingramcontent.com/pod-product-compliance
Lightning Source LLC
Chambersburg PA
CBHW071107050326
40690CB00008B/1144